Accounting Technician

INTERMEDIATE LEVEL
NVQ/SVQ 3

Unit 6

Recording and Evaluating Costs and Revenues

WORKBOOK

FOULKS LYNCH
PUBLICATIONS

British Library Cataloguing-in-Publication Data

A catalogue record for this book is available from the British Library.

Published by

AT Foulks Lynch Ltd
4, The Griffin Centre
Staines Road
Feltham
Middlesex
TW14 0HS

ISBN 0 7483 5949 4

Printed and bound in Great Britain by Ashford Colour Press Ltd, Gosport, Hants.

© AT Foulks Lynch Ltd, 2003

Acknowledgements

We are grateful to the Association of Accounting Technicians for permission to reproduce the 2003 specimen simulation and specimen examination.

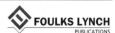

CONTENTS

FOULKS LYNCH
PUBLICATIONS

INTRODUCTION

This is the new edition of the AAT Workbook for Unit 6 – *Recording and Evaluating Costs and Revenues*.

Tailored to the new standards of competence, this workbook has been written specifically for AAT students in a clear and comprehensive style.

This workbook contains numerous practice activities, to reinforce the main topics you will need to prove your competence in. It also includes the specimen simulation and examination released by the AAT, which shows the kind questions you will be faced. In addition, there are further simulations covering various performance criteria for plently of practice before your actual assessment.

ASSESSMENT

Unit 6 is assessed by both **Skills Testing** and **Examination**.

Examination

The examination will be three hours long (plus 15 minutes reading time) and will include practical tests linked to the performance criteria and questions focusing on knowledge and understanding.

Section 1: This will assess your competence in elements 6.1 and 6.2. Tasks may include:

- methods of stock control and pricing of materials, including First In First Out, Last In First Out and Weighted Average Cost.
- preparing cost accounting entries for material, labour and overhead costs of the organisation
- calculating direct labour costs
- allocating and apportioning indirect costs to responsibility centres, including direct and step-down methods
- calculating departmental absorption rates using different absorption bases
- calculation product cost using absorption and marginal costing.

Section 2: This will assess your competence in element 6.3. Tasks may include:

- separating variable and fixed costs and the effect of changing capacity levels
- preparing estimates of future income and costs
- short-term planning tasks involving cost-volume-profit analysis for a single product
- product mix decisions using limiting factor analysis
- long-term planning tasks using net present value and payback techniques
- preparing a report.

Skills testing

Skills testing when your approved assessment centre (AAC) is a workplace

You may be observed carrying out your accounting activities as part of your normal work routine. You need to collect documentary evidence of the work you have done in an accounting portfolio.

Skills testing when your AAC is a college

This will use a combination of:

- documentary evidence of activities carried out at work, collected in a portfolio
- realistic simulations of workplace activities
- projects and assignments.

Skills testing when you don't work in accountancy

Don't worry – you can prove your competence using one of AAT's simulations, or from case studies, projects and assignments.

The AAT simulation

- The simulation will be four hours long, with an additional 15 minutes reading time.

- It will be based around a single scenario containing information relevant to all three elements of the unit.

- The simulation will be split into two parts, both taking two hours to complete. Part 1 will cover elements 6.1 and 6.2; part 2 will cover element 6.3.

- Any range statements or performance criteria not covered in the simulation will need to be tested in some other way, with the evidence of the additional testing going in your portfolio.

FOULKS LYNCH
PUBLICATIONS

PRACTICE ACTIVITIES

INTRODUCTION TO COST ACCOUNTING

ACTIVITY 1

(a)   Define the term Cost Unit.

(b)   Identify an appropriate Cost Unit for the following businesses or services.

Business/Service   *Cost Unit*

Airline

Accountant's practice

Office

Restaurant

Hospital

Limestone Quarry

Brewery

University

Oil Refinery

This activity covers performance criterion B in element 6.1.

ACTIVITY 2

The administrative cost related to the fleet of taxis based on three levels of annual mileage shows.

Mileage	Cost £
600,000	110,000
800,000	130,000
1,000,000	150,000

Identify the variable cost per mile and the fixed element of the total administrative costs.

This activity covers performance criteria C and D in element 6.3.

ORDERING AND ISSUING MATERIALS

ACTIVITY 3

Peter Bailes reviews his stock levels every six weeks. For one line of stock it is expected that 24 units will be required during each six week review period. Peter is concerned about stock-outs and therefore keeps a buffer stock of six units. At the last review there were only five units remaining in stock.

Assume that replacement stock is received immediately it is ordered.

Task

Calculate how many units Peter should order.

This activity covers performance criterion D in element 6.1.

ACTIVITY 4

Jacob Saunders expects to use 300 metres of wood in his business each week. He has the capacity to store 1,200 metres of wood in his workshop and this is to be the maximum level of wood stock that he holds. Jacob is concerned about running out of wood and therefore has decided to hold 300 metres of buffer stock.

Task

Calculate how often Jacob should review his levels of wood stock.

This activity covers performance criterion D in element 6.1.

ACTIVITY 5

KG Holdings has the following data relating to component 124

Re-order quantity 6,000 units.

Estimated usage per month:

Maximum 4,000

Minimum 1,000

Estimated lead times for supplier's delivery:

Maximum 6 days

Minimum 2 days

Task

Calculate the re-order level. Assume 25 working days per month.

This activity covers performance criterion D in element 6.1.

ACTIVITY 6

A retail shop purchases and sells microwave ovens. Each oven costs £140 and sells for £210. The cash used to purchase the oven would have earned 12% if left in the bank. If a microwave oven stays in stock for a year it is estimated that it incurs storage costs of £3.20.

Task

Calculate how much it costs to hold one oven in stock for one year.

This activity covers performance criterion D in element 6.1.

ACTIVITY 7

KG Holdings has the following data relating to component 125.

Re-order quantity 5,000 units.

Estimated usage per month:

Maximum   3,000

Minimum   1,000

Estimated lead times for supplier's delivery:

Maximum   5 days

Minimum   2 days

Task

Calculate the re-order level. Assume 25 working days per month.

This activity covers performance criterion D in element 6.1.

ACTIVITY 8

JK Manufacturing purchases a raw material SCS for use in its products. It estimates that each order costs £45 and annual holding costs are £1.50 per unit. Annual demand is expected to be 150,000 units

Task

Calculate the economic order quantity.

This activity covers performane criterion D in element 6.1.

ACTIVITY 9

A purchase order is to be raised for 100 litres of material JG571. It is to be purchased from Lynn Paul Ltd at a price of £16.75 per litre and delivered on 22 October 200X. The purchase requisition number for this material is P1114 and the purchase order is to be made on 5 October 200X and is number 71443.

Task

Complete the purchase order in accordance with these requirements.

PURCHASE ORDER				
To:		Number: Date: Purchase requisition number:		
Please supply in accordance with attached conditions of purchase.				
Quantity	Description/ code	Delivery date	Price £	Per
Origination department: Authorisation:				

This activity covers performance criterion B in element 6.1.

ACTIVITY 10

On 22 September 200X a company received 4,000 units of APB2 from Jones Material Supplies Ltd required by the factory. The materials were delivered by Smith Deliveries & Co and a sample of the boxes were inspected by the Stores Assistant Manager. The 40 boxes received containing the material were subsequently passed as suitable. The materials were checked against purchase order number 37523.

Task

Complete the goods received note (number 43719) for these boxes.

<table>
<tr><td colspan="4" align="center">**GOODS RECEIVED NOTE**</td></tr>
</table>

Supplier:		Number:
		Date:
Carrier:		Purchase order no:
Date of delivery		

Description	Code	Quantity	Number of packages

Received by:
Required by:
Accepted by:
Date:

INSPECTION REPORT

Quantity passed	Quantity rejected	Remarks

Inspector:
Date:

This activity covers performance criterion B in element 6.1.

ACTIVITY 11

On 22 October 200X a delivery was received by ABC Ltd of 100 litres of material JG571 from Lynn Paul Ltd. The purchase order for these goods was dated 5 October 200X and its serial number was 71443. The purchase invoice for these goods is to be sent by post and is to carry the serial number of 53533. The price of the goods was £16.75 per litre and payment is due in 14 days.

Task

Complete the purchase invoice using these details.

<table>
<tr><td colspan="2" align="center">**LYNN PAUL LTD – PURCHASE INVOICE**</td></tr>
<tr><td>To:
Date:
Purchase order no:</td><td>Number:</td></tr>
<tr><td>For supply and delivery of:

Payment due in 14 days</td><td>£</td></tr>
</table>

This activity covers performance criterion B in element 6.1.

ACTIVITY 12

The goods received note below shows 100 litres of material JG571 supplied by Lynn Paul Ltd at a price of £16.75 per litre.

ABC LTD GOODS RECEIVED			
Supplier: Lynn Paul Ltd		Number: 3325	
		Date: 22 Oct 20X1	
Carrier: Lynn Paul Deliveries		Purchase order no: 71443	
Date of delivery: 22 October 20X1			
Description	*Code*	*Quantity*	*Number of packages*
Material	JG571	100 litres	10
Received by: Stores Required by: Manufacturing Accepted by: Stores Manager Date: 22 October 20X1			

INSPECTION REPORT		
Quantity passed	*Quantity rejected*	*Remarks*
100 litres	-	-
Inspector: Stores Manager Date: 22 October 20X1		

Task

Use the goods received note to write up the stores ledger account for this material.

STORES LEDGER ACCOUNT										
Material...................................					Maximum quantity...............................					
Code..					Minimum quantity..............................					
Receipts					Issues				Stock		
Date	GRN No	Quantity	Unit price £	Amount £	Date	Stores No. Req	Quantity	Amount £	Quantity	Unit price £	Amount £

This activity covers performance criterion B in element 6.1.

ACTIVITY 13

The factory returns 2 metres of 4 cm hardwood (code HW400) on 15 May 200X as it is surplus to current requirements. The return is authorised by the factory manager and the wood is received by the storekeeper. The bin card is written up immediately but the stores ledger account is not written up until 20 May 200X.

Task

Write up the goods returned note, the bin card and the stores ledger account.

GOODS RETURNED NOTE			Ref: RET/86
Date returned	Description	Code	Quantity
Released by:			
Accepted by:			
Bin card entered:			
Stores ledger card entered:			

BIN CARD

Description.4cm.Hardwood.................Location.Stores.................. Code..HW400......

Maximum...............Minimum..............Reorder level............ Reorder quantity...........

Receipts			Issues			Current stock level	On order		
Date	GRN Ref	Quantity	Date	Issue Ref	Quantity		Date	Ref	Quantity

STORES LEDGER ACCOUNT

Material................................. Maximum quantity..

Code................................. Minimum quantity..

Receipts					Issues				Stock		
Date	GRN No	Quantity	Unit price £	Amount £	Date	Stores No. Req	Quantity	Amount £	Quantity	Unit price £	Amount £

This activity covers performance criterion B in element 6.1.

ACTIVITY 14

The following information relates to component BCD.

Maximum stock has been set at		5,500 units
Usage per month	Maximum	1,100 units
	Minimum	900 units
Estimated delivery period	Maximum	4 months
	Minimum	2 months

Task 1

Using the data below calculate:

(i) the re-order level

(ii)   the re-order quantity

(iii)   the minimum level

(iv)   the average stock held.

Task 2

What do you consider to be the essential practices of efficient storekeeping? Explain by giving at least four examples.

This activity covers performance criterion B in element 6.1.

ACTIVITY 15

Name the documents which you would consider important in the control and authorisation of material purchases.

This activity covers performance criterion E in element 6.1.

ACTIVITY 16

Describe the essential requirements of an effective material stock control system.

This activity covers performance criteria D and E in element 6.1.

ACTIVITY 17

An importer deals only in one commodity and has recorded the following transactions for the first six months of the year:

Purchases

Date	Quantity purchased	Gross invoice value £	Quantity discount units
1 February	100	30,000	Nil
1 March	200	60,000	2.5%
1 May	300	90,000	5%

Sales

Date	Quantity sold units	Total sales value £
February	75	30,000
May	350	175,000

There was an opening balance at 1 January of 50 units, valued at £12,500.

Task

Prepare the stores ledger account for the six months using the perpetual inventory system and:

(a)   the FIFO method of pricing issues

(b)   the LIFO method of pricing issues

(c)   the weighted average method of pricing issues.

This activity covers performance criteria A and C in element 6.1.

ACTIVITY 18

Wood & Bark Ltd trade in a single product and maintain a perpetual inventory. The company has valued its stock on the LIFO basis, but is now proposing to change to the FIFO method.

Their records disclose that 2,000 units were in stock at the beginning of the current period, and valued on the basis of a receipt of 5,000 units priced at £2.50 of which 4,000 had been sold before the end of the previous period, plus 500 from a delivery in 199Z when the cost was £2.00 per unit, plus 500 purchased in 199X when the cost was £0.50 per unit.

The following transactions took place in the period January 200X to June 200X:

January	Sold	1,500 units at £4.00 each
February	Received	10,000 units at £2.50 each
March	Sold	8,000 units at £4.00 each
April	Received	15,000 units at £2.60 each
May	Received	6,500 units at £2.70 each
June	Sold	22,000 units at £4.00 each

Task

Calculate the stock valuation at 30 June 200X using:

(i)   the LIFO method;

(ii)   the FIFO method.

This activity covers performance criteria A and C in element 6.1.

DIRECT LABOUR

ACTIVITY 19

An organisation pays its employees by results on the following basis:

Production per week	Rate per unit
Units	£
1 – 60	3.00
61 – 80	3.20
81 – 100	3.50
101 and above	3.80

FOULKS LYNCH PUBLICATIONS

Task

Calculate the two alternative amounts that could be paid for 89 units produced in a week depending upon the precise terms of the agreement.

This activity covers performance criterion C in element 6.1.

ACTIVITY 20

An employee is paid a basic hourly rate of £4.40 per hour. The overtime payments are 1½ times the hourly rate.

Task

Calculate the amount paid for each hour of overtime.

This activity covers performance criterion B in element 6.1.

ACTIVITY 21

A salaried employee is paid £16,400 per annum and is expected to work for at least 37.5 hours per week. He is paid for all 52 weeks of the year. Any additional hours are paid at an overtime rate of twice the normal hourly rate for this employee.

Task

If this employee works five hours of overtime in a month calculate how much he will be paid in addition to his basic salary.

This activity covers performance criterion B in element 6.1.

ACTIVITY 22

A division of a company has decided to pay an annual bonus to its 15 employees due to its good performance during the year.

Task

Calculate the bonus paid to an employee with an annual salary of £22,000 if the bonus is to be allocated on the basis of 2% of annual salary.

This activity covers performance criterion B in element 6.1.

ACTIVITY 23

Employee's basic rate	£4.80 per hour
Allowed time for job B	20 minutes
Time taken for job B	18 minutes

Task

Calculate the total payment to an employee from the above data using the Halsey bonus scheme.

This activity covers performance criterion C in element 6.1.

 **FOULKS LYNCH**
PUBLICATIONS

ACTIVITY 24

In a payments by results scheme employees are paid a bonus based on hours saved at the basic wage rate. The bonus payable to the employee is calculated as the hours saved multiplied by the ratio of time saved to time allowed.

An employee produces 480 units in 72 hours. The time allowed for this number of units is 108 hours. The employee's basic rate of pay is £5.40 per hour.

Task

Calculate the total amount payable to the employee for this job.

This activity covers performance criterion C in element 6.1.

ACTIVITY 25

Nessa Trandheim works in the production area of FG Toyles Ltd. Her clock card number is NT 641. She is paid an hourly rate of £4.80 for the work that she performs and she must record this work on a weekly time sheet. She works on one of three products J, K and L.

The standard working week for the company is 38 hours and any overtime is paid at twice the normal hourly rate.

During the week commencing 4 June Nessa worked the following hours:

Monday 4/6	9.00 am - 12.00	Product J
	1.00 pm - 7.00 pm	Product L
Tuesday 5/6	8.00 am - 12.00 pm	Product L
	1.00 pm - 6.00 pm	Product K
Wednesday 6/6	9.00 am - 12.00 pm	Product K
	1.00 pm - 5.00 pm	Product K
Thursday 7/6	8.00 am - 1.00 pm	Product K
	2.00 pm - 5.00 pm	Product K
Friday 8/6	8.00 am - 11.00 am	Product L
	12.30 pm - 5.30 pm	Product J

Task

Enter this information on to the following time sheet for Nessa for the week commencing 4 June.

TIME SHEET						
Name:				**Clock Number:**		
Department:						
Week commencing:						
To be completed by employee				For office use		
Day	*Start*	*Finish*	*Job*	*Code*	*Hours*	*£*
Monday						
Tuesday						
Wednesday						
Thursday						
Friday						
Basic pay						
Overtime premium						———
Gross wages						———
Foreman's signature:						
Date:						

This activity covers performance criterion B in element 6.1.

ACTIVITY 26

A group of six employees work on a particular batch of a product on a production line. In one particular day they work on two batches. One batch, number 239457, requires in total 25 hours of their labour at an average cost of £6.50 per hour and the second batch, number 239458, requires only 23 hours at an average cost of £6.50 per hour. Both batches also require the labour of additional employees who are paid by results. Their agreed payment is £2.50 per unit produced. Batch 239457 totals 27 units and batch 239458 totals 24 units.

Task

Record these details on cost cards for each batch number.

COST CARD – BATCH 239457	
	£
Materials cost	X
Labour cost	

COST CARD – BATCH 239458

	£
Materials cost	X
Labour cost	

This activity covers performance criterion B in element 6.1.

ACTIVITY 27

The time sheet for Rajesh Jabasi for the week commencing 28 March is given below. His clock number is 289464 and he works in stores as the assistant manager. All of his hours are charged to the stores department. The standard working week for his organisation is 35 hours, his annual salary is £20,020 and any overtime that he works is paid at time and a half.

TIME SHEET

Name: Rajesh Jabasi   **Clock Number:** 289464

Department: Stores

Week commencing: 28 March

Date	Job	Start	Finish	Hours	Overtime Hrs	£
28 March	Stores	9.00	1.00			
		1.30	5.30	8.0		
29 March	Stores	9.00	12.30			
		1.30	6.30	8.5		
30 March	Stores	8.00	2.00	6.0		
31 March	Stores	8.00	1.00			
		1.30	6.00	9.5		
1 April	Holiday	9.30	1.00			
		2.00	5.30	7.0		
				39.0	4	
Total overtime payment						66.00

Supervisor's signature ....

To be included in this week's wage payment is a bonus for the previous quarter totalling 0.6% of his annual salary.

Task

Record these details in the payroll for the week commencing 28 March.

Name	Clock No	Hrs	Pay				Deductions			
			Basic pay	Overtime premium	Bonus	Gross pay	Tax	NI	Other	Net pay
R Jabasi										

This activity covers performance criterion B in element 6.1.

ACTIVITY 28

The personnel department will maintain a personnel history record for each employee.

Task

Summarise the details you would expect to find in such a report.

ACTIVITY 29

The following information is available:

Normal working day	8 hours
Guaranteed rate of pay (on time basis)	£5.50 per hour
Standard time allowed to produce one unit	3 minutes
Piecework price	£0.1 per standard minute
Premium bonus	75% of time saved, in addition to hourly pay

Task

For the following levels of output produced in one day

80 units

120 units

210 units

calculate earnings based on:

(a) piecework, where earnings are guaranteed at 80% of time-based pay;

(b) premium bonus system.

This activity covers performance criterion C in element 6.1.

ACTIVITY 30

An organisation operates an individual premium bonus scheme in which an operator's performance is calculated and paid for as detailed below:

Each task is given a target expressed in standard minutes. The amount of weekly output achieved is stated as a total of standard minutes. The week's total of standard minutes is expressed as a percentage of attendance time (to the nearest whole number). The operator is paid:

FOULKS LYNCH
PUBLICATIONS

Percentage performance	Rate paid per hour
	£
0 - 75	4.20
76 - 90	4.40
91 - 110	4.80
111 and over	5.40

Three products are assembled and have the following standard times:

Product A - 42 standard minutes

Product B - 60 standard minutes

Product C - 75 standard minutes

Task

Calculate the gross pay for each operator from the following information:

Operator	Hours attended	Performance: products assembled		
		A	B	C
X	38	15	13	11
Y	39	15	10	8
Z	42	15	18	16

This activity covers performance criterion C in element 6.1.

ACTIVITY 31

The following data is available for an employee:

Basic rate	£4.80 per hour
Time allowed Job A	1 hour
Time taken Job A	36 minutes

Task

Calculate the total payment for Job A under both the Halsey and Rowan schemes.

This activity covers performance criterion C in element 6.1.

ACTIVITY 32

A Ltd makes engineering components. The company has been manufacturing 6,000 components per week, with six direct employees working a 40-hour work, at a basic wage of £4.00 per hour. Each worker operates independently.

A new remuneration scheme is being introduced. Each employee will receive payment on the following basis:

First 800 components per week	16 pence per unit
Next 200 components per week	17 pence per unit
All additional components per week	18 pence per unit

There will be a guaranteed minimum wage of £140.00 per week. It is expected that output will increase to 6,600 components per week with the new scheme.

Task

Describe the general features of time based and individual performance based remuneration systems, and outline the relative merits of each type of system.

(Use the above figures to illustrate your discussion, making whatever additional assumptions that you feel are necessary.)

This activity covers performance criterion A in element 6.1.

DIRECT AND INDIRECT EXPENSES

ACTIVITY 33

Task

Suggest the most appropriate cost unit for each of the following activities:

(a)   Engineering

(b)   Gas production

(c)   Steel production

(d)   Education

(e)   Sales and marketing

(f)   Telephone switchboard

This activity covers performance criterion C in element 6.1.

ACTIVITY 34

A company produces electronic circuit boards. Each circuit board has a raw material input of £60 and labour input that costs £20. The company must also pay the rent of the factory totalling £20,000 per annum, business rates of £4,000 per annum and the production director's salary of £24,000 per annum.

Task

Identify the variable costs and fixed costs of this business.

This activity covers performance criterion D in element 6.2, and C in element 6.3.

ACTIVITY 35

A machine has been used by a business for the last five years and it is estimated to have a further three years of life. The machine has so far been used for 5,400 hours and it is estimated to have a remaining life of 3,600 hours. The machine originally cost £47,000 and

it has been used during this year for 1,200 hours. The cost accounting depreciation charge is based upon machine hour rate.

Task

Calculate the depreciation charge for this year.

This activity covers performance criterion A in element 6.2.

ACTIVITY 36

Within the costing system of a manufacturing company the following types of expense are incurred:

Reference number

1	Cost of oils used to lubricate production machinery
2	Motor vehicle licences for lorries
3	Depreciation of factory plant and equipment
4	Cost of chemicals used in the laboratory
5	Commission paid to sales representatives
6	Salary of the secretary to the Finance Director
7	Trade discount given to customers
8	Holiday pay of machine operatives
9	Salary of security guard in raw material warehouse
10	Fees to advertising agency
11	Rent of finished goods warehouse
12	Salary of scientist in laboratory
13	Insurance of the company's premises
14	Salary of supervisor working in the factory
15	Cost of typewriter ribbons in the general office
16	Protective clothing for machine operatives

Task 1

Place each expense within the following classifications:

Production overhead

Selling and Distribution overhead

Administration overhead

Research and Development overhead

Each type of expense should appear only once in your answer. You may use the reference numbers in your answer.

Task 2

Give three reasons why direct production labour cost might be regarded as a fixed cost rather than as a variable cost.

This activity covers performance criterion A in element 6.1 and A in element 6.2.

ACTIVITY 37

Explain whether you agree with each of the following statements:

(a)   'All direct costs are variable'

(b)   'Variable costs are controllable and fixed costs are not'.

This activity covers performance criterion A in element 6.1.

APPORTIONMENT OF INDIRECT COSTS

ACTIVITY 38

You are given the following information about some overhead costs for an organisation:

Factory building insurance	£1,600
Machinery depreciation	£17,400
Maintenance department costs	£21,000

The organisation has two production departments in the factory building, X and Y, and the following information is also available:

	Dept X	Dept Y
Floor area	1,200 sq ft	400 sq ft
Value of machinery	£64,000	£32,000
Number of maintenance department call outs in period	12	24

Task

Apportion the overheads to departments X and Y.

This activity covers performance criterion B in element 6.2.

ACTIVITY 39

In the previous activity the overheads were apportioned to each of the five cost centres to give the following total overhead cost for each cost centre.

OVERHEAD ANALYSIS SHEET					DATE:	
	TOTAL	PRODUCTION			SERVICE	
	£	Assembly £	Machining £	Finishing £	Maint. £	Canteen £
Total overhead	60,000	19,050	16,275	11,437	5,175	8,063

Additional information regarding the organisation:

	Assembly	Machining	Finishing	Maintenance	Canteen
Number of employees	50	30	20	5	4
Floor space occupied (sq ft)	80	70	50	10	40
Machinery value (£'000)	200	180	50	20	30
Number of vehicles	3	1	5	10	1

Task 1

Using the following overhead analysis sheet, reapportion the service department costs. canteen costs are to be apportioned on the basis of number of employees in each production department and maintenance costs are to be apportioned on the basis of the value of machinery in each production department. Assume that the service cost centres do not service each other.

OVERHEAD ANALYSIS SHEET					DATE:	
	TOTAL	PRODUCTION			SERVICE	
	£	Assembly £	Machining £	Finishing £	Maint. £	Canteen £
Overheads						
Apportion maintenance						
Apportion canteen						

Task 2

Using the following overhead analysis sheet, reapportion the service department costs. Use the same basis of apportionment as for task 1, but this time assume that the service departments service each other.

OVERHEAD ANALYSIS SHEET				DATE:	
	TOTAL	PRODUCTION		SERVICE	
	£	Assembly £	Machining £	Finishing £	Maint. £	Canteen £
Overheads						
Apportion maintenance						
Apportion canteen						

This activity covers performance criterion B in element 6.2.

OVERHEAD ABSORPTION

ACTIVITY 40

An organisation has two production departments, cutting and assembly, and two products XJ1 and XJ2.

Information about the departments and products is as follows:

	Cutting	Assembly
Budgeted overhead	£67,000	£42,000
Labour hours for one unit of product XJ1	2.50	0.75
Labour hours for one unit of product XJ2	1.00	1.00

	Product XJ1	Product XJ2
Budgeted production (units)	20,000	10,000

Task

Calculate:

(i)   the overhead absorption rate per labour hour for each department

(ii)   the total amount of overhead to be included in the cost of each of the two products.

This activity covers performance criteria C and D in element 6.2.

ACTIVITY 41

An organisation produces two products, X and Y, in two production departments, I and II. Materials are input into the products in both departments. Details of the departments and the products are as follows:

	Production departments	
	I	II
Total standard overhead	£46,000	£75,000

	Product	
	X	Y
Standard direct material input per unit:		
Department I	£1.20	£24.50
Department II	£9.30	£10.80
Number of products to be produced	10,000	6,000

Task

Calculate:

(i)   the overhead absorption rate on the basis of standard direct materials cost

(ii)   the amount of overhead included for each of the two products.

This activity covers performance criteria C and D in element 6.2.

ACTIVITY 42

An organisation produces two products, J and K, in three production departments. The production departments are as follows:

Machine shop	machine based
	machine hour overhead absorption rate to be used
	total expected overhead £269,000
Polishing department	labour based
	labour hour overhead absorption rate to be used
	total expected overhead £240,000
Finishing department	variety of labour grades used
	total labour cost overhead absorption rate to be used
	total expected overhead £170,000

Details of the production of the two products are as follows:

Product J (per unit)

Machine hours	machine shop 4 hours
	polishing 1 hour
	finishing 0.5 hours

Labour hours:

Machine shop	grade F 1 hour
	grade G 0.5 hours
Polishing	grade D 3 hours
	grade F 1 hour
Finishing	grade B 8 hours
	grade C 1 hour

Product K (per unit)

Machine hours	machine shop 6 hours
	polishing 2 hours
	finishing 2 hours

Labour hours:

Machine shop	grade D 2 hours
	grade C 1 hour
Polishing	grade D 3 hours
Finishing	grade C 6 hours
	grade A 2 hours

The hourly rates of pay for each of the labour grades is as follows:

Grade A	£10.10
Grade B	£8.70
Grade C	£6.40
Grade D	£5.00
Grade E	£4.00
Grade F	£3.60
Grade G	£3.00

It is anticipated that 20,000 units of product J and 30,000 units of product K will be produced.

Task

Calculate the amount of overhead to be included in the cost of each of the products J and K.

This activity covers performance criteria C and D in element 6.2.

ACTIVITY 43

Budgeted overhead	£14,000
Actual overhead	£12,000
Budgeted hours	28,000
Actual hours	25,000

Task

From the above information calculate any under or over absorption of overheads and show what factors have caused the under or over absorption.

This activity covers performance criterion E in element 6.2.

ACTIVITY 44

The following details relate to the production of books by a publishing company, Whetstone Ltd:

Production area	Print	Binding	Jacket & finishing
Machine hours (mh) or labour hours (lh)	20,000mh	30,000lh	5,000lh
Annual overhead cost	£8,000	£12,000	£6,000

The book has direct costs of

Print	£1.50
Binding	£0.75
Jacket	£0.30

It spends 15 minutes being printed, 30 minutes being bound and 15 minutes in the jacket and finishing department.

Task

Work out a product cost for one book which passes through the three production departments.

This activity covers performance criteria C in element 6.1 and D in element 6.2.

ACTIVITY 45

Bookdon plc manufactures three products in two production departments, a machine shop and a fitting section; it also has two service departments, a canteen and a machine maintenance section. Shown below are next year's budgeted production data and manufacturing costs for the company.

Product	X	Y	Z
Production	4,200 units	6,900 units	1,700 units
Prime cost			
Direct materials	£11 per unit	£14 per unit	£17 per unit
Direct labour			
Machine shop	£6 per unit	£4 per unit	£2 per unit
Fitting section	£12 per unit	£3 per unit	£21 per unit
Machine hours, per unit	6 hours per unit	3 hours per unit	4 hours per unit

	Machine shop	Fitting section	Canteen	Machine maintenance section	Total
	£	£	£	£	£
Allocated overheads	27,660	19,470	16,600	26,650	90,380
Rent, rates, heat and light					17,000
Depreciation and insurance of equipment					25,000

Additional data

Gross book value of equipment	150,000	75,000	30,000	45,000
Number of employees	18	14	4	4
Floor space occupied - square metres	3,600	1,400	1,000	800

It has been estimated that approximately 70% of the machine maintenance section's costs are incurred servicing the machine shop and the remainder incurred servicing the fitting section.

Task

Calculate:

(i)   the following budgeted overhead absorption rates:

(1)   a machine hour rate for the machine shop; and

(2)   a rate expressed as a percentage of direct wages for the fitting section

All working and assumptions should be clearly shown.

(ii)   the budgeted manufacturing overhead cost per unit of product X.

This activity covers performance criteria B and D in element 6.2.

ACTIVITY 46

An industrial concern manufactures three products known as P, Q and R. Each product is started in the machining area and completed in the finishing shop. The direct costs associated with each product forecast for the next trading period are:

	P	Q	R
	£	£	£
Materials	18.50	15.00	22.50
Wages			
Machining area at £5 per hour	10.00	5.00	10.00
Finishing shop at £4 per hour	6.00	4.00	8.00
	34.50	24.00	40.50

There are machines in both departments and machine hours required to complete one of each product are:

	P	Q	R
Machine area	4	1.5	3
Finishing shop	0.5	0.5	1
Budget output in units	6,000	8,000	2,000

Fixed overheads are		
Machine area	£100,800	
Finishing shop	£94,500	

Task 1

Calculate an overhead absorption rate for fixed overheads using:

(i)   a labour hour rate for each department

(ii)   a machine hour rate for each department.

Task 2

Calculate the total cost of each product using:

(i)   the labour hour rate

(ii)   the machine hour rate,

as calculated in Task 1 above.

Task 3

Write down your comments to the factory manager who has suggested that one overhead rate for both departments would simplify matters.

This activity covers performance criteria C and D in element 6.2.

CODING AND ACCOUNTING FOR COSTS

ACTIVITY 47

The overheads of an international organisation are coded with a seven digit code system as follows:

First and second digits	location
Third and fourth digits	function
Final three digits	type of expense

Extracts from within the costing system are as follows:

Location	Code
London	10
Dublin	11
Lagos	12
Nairobi	13
Kuala Lumpur	17
Hong Kong	18

Type of expense	Code
Factory rent	201
Plant depreciation	202
Stationery	203

 FOULKS LYNCH
PUBLICATIONS

Telephone	204
Travel	207
Entertainment	209

Function	*Code*
Production	20
Marketing	21
Accounts	23
Administration	24

Examples of the codes are as follows:

Factory rent in Nairobi:	1320201
Stationery purchased in London office:	1024203

Task 1

State the codes for the following items:

(a)   Depreciation of plant in the Dublin factory.

(b)   Administration telephone costs incurred in Lagos.

(c)   Salesman in Hong Kong entertaining an overseas visitor.

Task 2

State two advantages of using a coding system for the classification of costs and revenues.

This activity covers performance criterion A in element 6.2.

ACTIVITY 48

The following is a simple example of how a code may be made up.

Type of material (Generic class)

1XX   Raw materials

2XX   Oils and lubricants

3XX   Indirect materials

Specific types of material within a generic class

X1X   Timber

X2X   Glue

X4X   Machine oil Grade 1

X5X   Machine oil Grade 2

X7X   Packaging material

X8X   Stationery

X9X   Petrol

Departmental utilisation (functional class)

XX1   Production - assembly

XX2   Production - packaging department

XX3   Sales department

XX4   Accounts department

Code 111   would represent wood used as a raw material in assembly production.

Code 252   would represent Grade 2 machine oil used to lubricate machines in the packaging department.

Task

What would codes 384, 293 and 172 represent?

This activity covers performance criterion A in element 6.2.

ACTIVITY 49

At 1 July a manufacturing company had the following balances brought forward in its cost ledger accounts:

	£
Bank account	18,500
Stores ledger control account	2,125
Finished goods stock control account	1,500
Work in progress control account	2,000

Task

You are required to open ledger accounts for the above items in the cost ledger, post the following items which occurred in the period up to 31 October and open up other accounts as considered necessary including a costing profit and loss account.

		£
(a)	Stock materials purchased	12,000
(b)	Stock materials issued to production	12,500
(c)	Stock materials issued to maintenance department	1,000
(d)	Wages - direct	10,830
(e)	Included in direct wages is indirect work	600
(f)	Factory overheads incurred	4,200
(g)	Factory overheads absorbed into production	5,800
(h)	Work transferred to finished stock, at cost	24,000
(i)	Factory cost of sales	22,500
(j)	Sales at selling price	28,750
(k)	Administrative and selling costs (to be written off against profits)	4,250

This activity covers performance criteria B in element 6.1 and A in element 6.2.

FOULKS LYNCH
PUBLICATIONS

ACTIVITY 50

Handels has recently appointed a stores controller who has decided to introduce a new stores control system. He has asked you to design for him a new material code.

Task 1

(a) Briefly:

    (i) describe the principles you feel should be observed when designing a materials classification code

    (ii) state the advantages of such a coding in a system of stores control.

(b) Assume that the design of your coding system has been completed. Included in the range of Handels' products is a series of flat sections of varying dimensions and in four different raw materials - aluminium (01), brass (02), copper (03) and stainless steel (04). Examples of coding of two of these are:

Material	Dimensions			Code no.
	Length	*Thickness*	*Width*	
Stainless steel	4'	$\frac{7}{8}$ "	$3\frac{3}{4}$ "	04081415
Brass	8'6"	$1\frac{3}{8}$ "	2"	02172208

Interpret the coding system from the two codes given.

Task 2

Determine the code for the following:

    Aluminium $6'6" \times \frac{1}{4}" \times 3\frac{1}{2}"$

    Copper $1' \times \frac{3}{8}" \times 3\frac{1}{4}"$

Task 3

Describe the type of bar as defined by these codes:

    01112903

    03071721

This activity covers performance criterion B in element 6.1.

JOB AND BATCH COSTING

ACTIVITY 51

Task

Explain the difference between job costing and batch costing.

PROCESS COSTING

ACTIVITY 52

4,000 tonnes of material are input to a process where the normal loss is expected to be 4% of input. The output from the process was 3,800 tonnes.

Task

Calculate the abnormal loss.

This activity covers performance criterion A in element 6.3.

ACTIVITY 53

5,000 tonnes of raw material are input to process A, where the normal loss is expected to be 5% of the input. The output from the process was 4,900 tonnes.

Task

Calculate the abnormal gain.

This activity covers performance criterion A in element 6.3.

ACTIVITY 54

Euromix produce a product which passes through a single process.

For the month of January X3 the following information relates to the process.

Input 3,000 litres of raw material at £2 litre.

Direct labour 160 hours at £7.50 per labour hour.

Process overhead £15 per labour hour.

Waste material has a residual value of £0.30 per litre.

Normal loss is expected to be 5% of input. Output for the period was 2,750 litres.

Task

Prepare the process account for the month; together with the normal and abnormal loss account.

This activity covers performance criterion A in element 6.3.

ACTIVITY 55

The following information relates to Euromix for the month of February X3.

Input 3,500 litres of raw material at £2 per litre.

Direct labour 160 hours at £7.50 per labour hour.

Process overhead £15 per labour hour.

Waste material has a residual value of £0.30 per litre.

Normal loss is expected to be 5% of input. Output for the period was 3,425 litres.

Task

Prepare the process account for the month; together with the normal loss and abnormal gain account.

This activity covers performance criterion A in element 6.3.

MARGINAL COSTING

ACTIVITY 56

The following information is a summary of the accounts of Yorkscoast Ltd for six months ended 30 June 20X1.

Sales	£252,000
Direct materials	£6,000
Direct labour	£45,000
Variable production overhead	£25,000
Fixed production overhead	£35,000
Variable selling distribution and administrative costs	£37,500
Fixed selling distribution and administrative costs	£25,000

Task

Prepare operating statements for the period based on absorption and marginal costing formats.

This activity covers performance criterion A in element 6.3.

ACTIVITY 57

Hockeystrike manufacture hockey sticks.

Its standard product 'H1' has the following specification.

Selling price per unit	£95.00
Direct labour/unit	£15.00
Direct material/unit	£20.00
Variable overhead/unit	£5.00

It plans to produce 1000 units in January X1, and to sell 900 units in the same period. There are no opening stocks of finished goods. Fixed costs for the period £25,000.

Task

Prepare operating statements for the period using both absorption and marginal costing principles.

This activity covers performance criterion A in element 6.3.

CVP ANALYSIS, BREAK-EVEN ANALYSIS AND THE LIMITING FACTOR

ACTIVITY 58

Using the cost and revenue specification in the example of Raw Feeds above calculate:

- Break-even point per month in tonnage.

- The % margin of safety, if the new business and a capacity of 100% was utilised.

This activity covers performance criteria B and C in element 6.3.

ACTIVITY 59

Raw Feeds plan for six months ended 30 June X1 was:

	£
Sales	2,780,000
Variable costs	2,700,000
Contribution	1,180,000
Fixed costs	360,000
Profit for period	£820,000

The company is working at 100% capacity.

Task

- Calculate by formula the break-even value of sales for the period.

- Prepare a profit volume graph to show the % level of activity at which the business breaks even.

This activity covers performance criteria B and C in element 6.3.

ACTIVITY 60

If Raw Feeds had a target profit of £1m for the six months ended 30 June X1 and its selling price and variable costs per unit were £105 and £75 but its fixed costs were revised to £375,000.

Task

Calculate the level of output and sales volume required to achieve the target profit.

This activity covers performance criteria B and C in element 6.3.

INVESTMENT APPRAISAL

ACTIVITY 60

Ravenscar Chemical Ltd are considering investing in a new machine for the blending process.

The capital cost of the equipment will be £125,000 and it will have a useful economic life of five years and will have no residual value.

The machine will increase the productive capacity of the plant and the additional cash flows over the next five years generated from increased business will be:

YR	1	£40,000
	2	£60,000
	3	£30,000
	4	£30,000
	5	£25,000

The company has a cost of capital of 15% and uses this to appraise new projects.

Task

Determine the payback period for the project and calculate the net present value.

NPV factors (15%)

YR	1	0.870
	2	0.757
	3	0.658
	4	0.573
	5	0.498

This activity covers performance criteria D and F in element 6.3.

ACTIVITY 62

Considering your answer to question 1, state whether or not you would recommend that management invest in the project.

FOULKS LYNCH
PUBLICATIONS

SPECIMEN SIMULATION

COVERAGE OF PERFORMANCE CRITERIA AND RANGE STATEMENTS

All performance criteria are covered in this simulation.

Element	PC coverage	Task(s)
6.1	**Record and analyse information relating to direct costs and revenues**	
A	Identify **direct costs** in accordance with the organisation's costing procedures.	1, 4
B	Record and analyse information relating to direct costs.	1, 4
C	Calculate direct costs in accordance with the organisation's policies and procedures.	2, 4
D	Check cost information for **stock** against usage and stock control practices.	3, 5
E	Resolve or refer queries to the appropriate person.	3
6.2	**Record and analyse information relating to the allocation, apportionment and absorption of overhead costs**	
A	Identify **overhead costs** in accordance with the organisation's procedures.	6
B	Attribute overhead costs to production and service cost centres in accordance with agreed **bases of allocation and apportionment**.	6
C	Calculate overhead absorption rates in accordance with agreed **bases of absorption**.	6, 7
D	Record and analyse information relating to overhead costs in accordance with the organisation's procedures.	7
E	Make adjustments for under and over recovered overhead costs in accordance with established procedures.	10
F	Review methods of allocation, apportionment and absorption at regular intervals in discussions with senior staff, and ensure agreed changes to methods are implemented.	8, 9
G	Consult staff working in operational departments to resolve any queries in overhead cost data.	10

6.3	Prepare and evaluate estimates of costs and revenues	
A	Identify information relevant to estimating current and future revenues and costs.	11
B	Prepare **estimates** of future income and costs.	11
C	Calculate the effects of variations in capacity on product costs.	11, 12
D	Analyse critical factors affecting costs and revenues using appropriate accounting techniques and draw clear conclusions from the analysis.	12
E	State any assumptions used when evaluating future costs and revenues.	12
F	Identify and evaluate options and solutions for their contribution to organisational goals.	12, 13
G	**Present** recommendations to appropriate people in a clear and concise way and supported by a clear rationale.	12, 13

Any missing range statements should be assessed separately.

PART 1

THE SITUATION

Your name is Bobby Forster and you work as the Accounts Assistant for Quality Candles Limited. The company manufactures candles of all kinds, including hand made candles. The candles are sold to wholesalers, to retailers, and direct to the public through the company's mail order division.

THE MANUFACTURING OPERATIONS

The manufacturing operations involve three production cost centres and two service cost centres.

Production cost centres	*Service cost centres*
Manufacturing	Stores
Painting and finishing	Maintenance
Packing	

THE TIME PERIOD COVERED BY THIS SIMULATION

The company's year end is 31 December. This simulation is concerned with activities during the quarter ending 31 December 20X3, and with planning activities for the year ending 31 December 20X4.

THE TASKS TO BE COMPLETED (PART ONE)

Element 6.1 (one hour)

TASK 1   Refer to the stores record card in the answer tables (item 13).

- Complete this stores record card using the information from the materials documentation (item 14 and item 1). You will need to identify and apply the stock valuation method in use and you are advised that VAT is not entered in the cost accounting records.

- Show the volume and value of the stock at the close of the week ending 10 October 20X3. Any returns from production cost centres to stores are valued at the price of the most recent batch issued from stores.

TASK 2   Refer to the materials requisition note and materials returned note (item 14).

- Complete the column headed 'Cost office use only' on each of the two documents.

TASK 3   Refer to your completed stores record card (item 13).

- Prepare a memo for the general manager, drawing attention to any unusual issues concerning the stock levels for this item during the week. Your memo should highlight the issues, point out any possible consequences, and suggest any action that might be taken to prevent the unusual situations occurring.

TASK 4   Refer to the internal policy document (item 2) and the piecework operation card (item 15).

- Complete the piecework operation card using the information provided. You will need to do the following:

    - Calculate the piecework payment for each day.

    - Calculate any bonus payable for the day.

    - Calculate the total wages payable for the day.

    - Complete the analysis of total wages payable for the week.

TASK 5   Refer to the piecework operation card (item 15).

- Identify any possible discrepancy in the activity data and write a memo to the supervisor, Roy Hart, explaining clearly what you think the discrepancy might be.

Element 6.2 (one hour)

TASK 6   Refer to the memo from the general manager (item 3)

- Perform the production overhead allocation and apportionment exercise using the analysis sheet (item 16). You will see that the task has already been started in respect of indirect labour. The data that you have gathered can be found in item 4.

TASK 7   Refer to the memo from the general manager (item 5).

- Calculate the production overhead absorption rates for 20X4. You will need to make use of the following:

    - The data in item 4

    - Your results for the total production department overhead for 20X4 in item 16.

All absorption rates should be calculated to the nearest penny.

TASK 8   Refer to the memo from the general manager (item 6).

- Re-calculate the total production overhead for each production department, reversing the order of apportionment of the service department overheads. You will need to do the following:

    - Transfer your figures for total department overhead for all five departments from your overhead analysis sheet (item 16)

    - Re-apportion the service department overheads, apportioning the stores costs first to the other four departments on the basis of the

number of material requisitions. Then re-apportion the total overhead of the maintenance department to the three production departments, on the basis of maintenance hours.

Perform all calculations to the nearest £000.

TASK 9   Review your results from task 8 and write a memo to the general manager. In your memo you should:

- comment on the effect of the change in method;

- explain whether you think it is necessary to instigate a change in the method of re-apportionment of service department costs.

TASK 10   Refer to the memo and the production overhead data – item 7 and 8.

- Complete the journal entry form (item 17).

- Write a memo to the production manager detailing any queries concerning the data and suggesting possible causes of any discrepancies you have identified.

ITEM 1

<table>
<tr><td colspan="2" style="text-align:center">

SALES INVOICE
Threadshop Limited
25 Lyme Street, Taunton, TA2 4RP
</td></tr>
<tr><td>

Invoice to:
Quality Candles Limited

2 Norman Lane
Winterbury
RT5 8UT
</td><td>

VAT
Registration: 254 1781 26
Date/tax point: 9 October 20X3
Invoice number: T543
Your order: 47346
</td></tr>
</table>

DESCRIPTION OF GOODS/SERVICES	Total (£)
Candlewick thread, 200 metre rolls 80 rolls @ £2.38	190.40

Checked against GRN no:	427
Date received:	9 October 20X3
Signed	J Jones

Goods total	190.40
VAT @ 17.5%	33.32
Total due	**223.72**
Terms: net 30 days	

ITEM 2

INTERNAL POLICY DOCUMENT

Document no: 18

Subject: Wages

Issued: August 20X3

Piecework scheme

A piecework scheme is to be introduced into the manufacturing department in order to reward efficient and productive operatives.

A piecework rate per batch of **£0.50** will be paid for each batch of accepted output produced during a day.

In addition a bonus will be paid of 4 per cent of the piecework payment for any day on which the number of batches rejected by Quality Control is **less than 5 per cent** of the total number of batches produced.

A **guaranteed daily wage of £50** is payable if the piecework payment + bonus amounts to less than £50 in any day.

Analysis of wages

Piecework payments and guaranteed daily wages paid will be treated as direct wages costs.

Bonus payments will be treated as indirect wages costs.

Discrepancies on piecework operation cards

The company wishes to pay wages and report labour rates promptly. Therefore employees will initially be paid for the total wages calculated according to the data contained on the weekly piecework operation card.

Any discrepancies on operation cards will be referred to the supervisor. Any alterations to wages will be agreed with the employee before adjustment is made to the next wage payment.

ITEM 3

INTERNAL MEMO

To: Bobby Forster, Accounts Assistant

From: General Manager

Subject: Budgeted production costs for 20X4

Date: 28 October 20X3

As you know we have begun our budgetary planning exercise for 20X4.

I understand that you have been working on the analysis of budgeted production costs. Could you please pull together all the information you have gathered and carry out the allocation and apportionment exercise for production overhead costs for 20X4.

Thanks. Then we will have the necessary information that we need to calculate the pre-determined overhead absorption rates for 20X4.

ITEM 4

DATA FOR PRODUCTION OVERHEAD ANALYSIS FOR 20X4

1   Summary of budgeted production costs for 20X4

	£000
Direct materials	200
Indirect materials	40
Direct labour	420
Indirect labour:	
Manufacturing department	22
Painting and finishing department	14
Packing department	11
Stores	35
Maintenance	16
Rent and rates	105
Protective clothing	31
Power	40
Insurance	24
Heat and light	35
Depreciation	48
Other production overheads	15
	———
Total budgeted production costs	1,056

2   Other data

	Manufacturing	Painting/ finishing	Packing	Stores	Mainten-ance
Direct materials cost (£000)	150	25	25	-	-
Floor area (000 sq metres)	30	10	16	8	6
Power usage (%)	50	10	30	5	5
Net book value of equipment (£000)	220	80	120	40	20
Maintenance hours (000)	7	4	3	1	-
Materials requisitions (000)	18	10	9	-	11
Direct labour hours (000)	20	28	10	-	-
Machine hours (000)	200	14	90	-	-

3   Company procedures for the allocation and apportionment of production overheads

- 30 per cent of the total indirect materials cost is apportioned to stores and 30 per cent to maintenance. The remaining 40 per cent is apportioned to the production departments according to the direct materials cost.

- Rent and rates and heating and lighting costs are apportioned according to the floor area occupied by each department.

- The cost of protective clothing is allocated to the manufacturing department.

- Power costs are apportioned according to the power usage in each department.

- Insurance and depreciation costs are apportioned according to the net book value of equipment in each department.

- Other production overheads are apportioned equally to the production departments.

- The total cost of the maintenance department is apportioned to the other four departments according to the number of maintenance hours.

- After a charge has been received from the maintenance department, the total cost of the stores department is apportioned to the three production departments according to the number of material requisitions.

- All calculations are rounded to the nearest £000.

ITEM 5

INTERNAL MEMO

To: Bobby Forster, Accounts Assistant

From: General Manager

Subject: Pre-determined overhead absorption rates

Date: 28 October 20X3

Many thanks for all your hard work on the overhead analysis.

Could you please now use the results of your analysis to calculate overhead absorption rates for the three production departments for 20X4. We have decided that the most appropriate bases of absorption will be as follows:

- Manufacturing department: machine hour rate;

- Painting and finishing department: labour hour rate;

- Packing department: machine hour rate.

Thanks for your help.

ITEM 6

INTERNAL MEMO

To: Bobby Forster, Accounts Assistant

From: General Manager

Subject: Re-apportionment of service department costs

Date: 4 November 2003

I have been giving some thought to the method that we use to re-apportion the service department costs to the production departments.

As you know, at present it is our policy to apportion the maintenance costs to all cost centres before we re-apportion the total stores costs to the production cost centres.

I would like to see the effect of altering the order of re-apportionment of service department costs. Could you please rework the figures so that we can review the results?

Let me have the results and your views as soon as possible, please.

ITEM 7

INTERNAL MEMO
To: Bobby Forster, Accounts Assistant
From: General Manager
Subject: Overhead absorption for October 20X3
Date: 8 November 20X3
As you know it is company policy to accumulate the under or over-absorbed production overhead each month in an account maintained for this purpose.
The production overhead data for October 20X3 has now been finalised.
Could you please complete the journal entry for the absorption of production overhead into the work in progress accounts and transfer any under or over absorption for the month. Complete the entries using the data provided, but please let the production manager know if you have any queries concerning the data.

ITEM 8

Summary of production overhead data for October 20X3

	£
Actual production overhead incurred	15,800
Production overhead to be absorbed into work in progress	
Manufacturing department	18,500
Painting and finishing department	7,400
Packing department	8,300

PART 2

THE SITUATION

Your name is Bobby Forster and you work as the Accounts Assistant for Quality Candles Limited. The company manufactures candles of all kinds, including hand made candles. The candles are sold to wholesalers, to retailers, and direct to the public through the company's mail order division.

The manufacturing operations

The manufacturing operations involve three production cost centres and two service cost centres.

Production cost centre	Service cost centres
Manufacturing	Stores
Painting and finishing	Maintenance
Packing	

The time period covered by this simulation

The company's year end is 31 December. This simulation is concerned with activities during the quarter ending 31 December 20X3, and with planning activities for the year ending 31 December 20X4.

THE TASKS TO BE COMPLETED (PART TWO)

Element 6.3 (two hours)

TASK 11   Refer to the memo (item 9) and prepare the necessary information in response to the general manager's query. You will need to do the following.

- Use the data (item 10) to identify the cost and revenue behaviour patterns to be used in your projections.

- Use your identified cost and revenue behaviour patterns to complete the planned profit projection (item 18).

TASK 12   Refer to the memo (item 11) answer the General Manager's queries. You will need to do the following.

(i)   Use your identified cost and revenue behaviour patterns, adjusted for the change in materials cost, to prepare a revised planned profit statement for December. Complete the profit statement (item 19). There is space for your workings at the bottom of this page.

(ii)   Calculate the breakeven point in terms of the number of cases to be sold in December if the bulk discount is accepted. Round your answer up to the nearest number of whole cases. Also use the same working paper to calculate the margin of safety. Express your answer as a percentage of the increased planned activity for December.

(iii)   Prepare a memo to the general manager evaluating the results of your calculations. Your memo should contain the following:

- Your comments on the resulting profit, breakeven point and margin of safety

- A statement of any assumptions you have used in evaluating the proposal.

TASK 13   Refer to the memo – item 12 – and do the following:

(i)   Use the working paper (item 19) to calculate the payback period and the net present value of the proposed investment. Ignore inflation and perform all monetary calculations to the nearest £.

(ii)   Write a memo to the General Manager evaluating the proposal from a financial viewpoint and stating any assumptions you have made in your analysis.

ITEM 9

INTERNAL MEMO

To: Bobby Forster, Accounts Assistant

From: General Manager

Subject: Mail order division: revised plan for December 20X3

Date: 9 November 20X3

Could you please prepare the revised cost and revenue plan for the mail order division for December.

The plan is to sell 6,800 cases of candles and we will base our projections on the cost and revenue behaviour patterns experienced during August to October.

Thanks for your help.

ITEM 10

Quality Candles Limited: mail order division

Actual results for August to October 20X3

	August	September	October
Number of cases sold	7,000	6,200	5,900
	£	£	£
Candles cost	9,100	8,060	7,670
Packing materials cost	5,250	4,650	4,425
Packing labour cost	2,100	1,860	1,770
Packing overhead cost	5,400	5,240	5,180
Other overhead cost	2,500	*3,000	2,500
Total costs	24,350	22,810	21,545
Sales revenue	28,000	24,800	23,600
Profit	3,650	1,990	2,055

*   Other overhead cost was £500 higher than usual during September owing to an unexpected machine breakdown which necessitated the hire of a packing machine to maintain production. This event will not recur in the future.

ITEM 11

INTERNAL MEMO

To: Bobby Forster, Accounts Assistant

From: General Manager

Subject: Mail order division: bulk discounts for December 20X3

Date: 10 November 20X3

Many thanks for your splendid work on the cost and revenue projections for December.

We are looking for opportunities to increase profit and we have just heard that we can obtain a bulk discount for packing materials in December if we increase our activity level to 7,600 cases for the month. This will mean that packing material unit costs will reduce by 20 per cent.

Could you please recalculate the profit projection for December if we decide to increase activity to take advantage of the discount?

Also, please calculate the breakeven point in terms of the number of cases to be sold in December if we make this change. I would also like to have a note of the margin of safety we will have.

Please let me have the results of your calculations and your comments on the outcome as soon as you can.

ITEM 12

INTERNAL MEMO

To: Bobby Forster, Accounts Assistant

From: General Manager

Subject: Purchase of delivery vehicles for mail order division

Date: 12 November 20X3

We are considering the purchase and operation of our own fleet of delivery vehicles at the end of this year.

The distribution manager informs me that we will be able to cancel our current delivery contract and as a result we will enjoy cash savings of £34,800 each year from 20X4 onwards, after taking account of the vehicle operating costs.

The vehicles will cost us £90,000 and will have a resale value of £5,000 when they are sold at the end of 20X7.

Can you please appraise this proposal from a financial viewpoint? I need to know the payback period and the net present value at our usual discount rate of 12 per cent. As you know our minimum required payback period for all capital projects is three years.

Please let me have the results as soon as possible.

ANSWER TABLES

ITEM 13 (for Task 1)

STORES RECORD CARD

Materials description:	Candlewick thread, 200 metre rolls	Maximum quantity: 400
Code no:	CW728	Minimum quantity: 140
		Reorder level: 230
		Reorder quantity: 80

Date 20X3	Receipts				Issues				Stock balance		
	Document number	Qty	Price per roll (£)	Total (£)	Document number	Qty	Price per roll (£)	Total (£)	Qty	Price per roll (£)	Total (£)
1 Oct									28	2.20	61.60
									26	2.30	59.80
									54		121.40
3 Oct					249	26	2.30	59.80			
						4	2.20	8.80			
						30		68.60	24	2.20	52.80
6 Oct	419	80	2.35	188.00					24	2.20	52.80
									80	2.35	188.00
									104		240.80

ITEM 14 (for Tasks 1 and 2)

<table>
<tr><td colspan="4" align="center">**MATERIALS REQUISITION**</td></tr>
<tr><td>Department:</td><td>Manufacturing</td><td>Document no:
Date:</td><td align="right">252
08/10/20X3</td></tr>
<tr><td>no</td><td>Description</td><td>Quantity</td><td>**Cost office use only**
Value of issue (£)</td></tr>
<tr><td>CW728</td><td>Candlewick thread, 200m rolls</td><td>40</td><td></td></tr>
<tr><td>Signature:</td><td></td><td colspan="2">Received by:</td></tr>
</table>

<table>
<tr><td colspan="4" align="center">**MATERIALS RETURNED**</td></tr>
<tr><td>Department:</td><td>Manufacturing</td><td>Document no:
Date:</td><td align="right">275
10/10/20X3</td></tr>
<tr><td>no</td><td>Description</td><td>Quantity</td><td>**Cost office use only**
Value of issue (£)</td></tr>
<tr><td>CW728</td><td>Candlewick thread, 200m rolls</td><td>3</td><td></td></tr>
<tr><td>Signature:</td><td></td><td colspan="2">Received by:</td></tr>
</table>

ITEM 15 (for Task 4)

QUALITY CANDLES LIMITED
PIECEWORK OPERATION CARD

Operative name: Mary Roberts   Department: Manufacturing

Clock number: R27

Week beginning: 6 October 20X3

	Mon	Tues	Wed	Thurs	Fri
Batches produced	120	102	34	202	115
Batches rejected	5	7	4	11	5
Batches accepted					
Rate per batch	£ 0.50	£ 0.50	£ 0.50	£ 0.50	£ 0.50
Piecework payment		£	£	£	£
Bonus payable	£	£	£	£	£
Total payable for day*		£	£	£	£

Total wages payable for week:

£

Direct wages

Indirect wages

Total wages   _____
                     _____

* Guaranteed daily wage of £50 is payable if piecework payment plus bonus amounts to less than £50.

Supervisor's signature: A Peters

ITEM 16 (for Task 5)

Production overhead analysis sheet for 20X4

Production overhead item	Total £000	Manufacturing £000	Painting/ finishing £000	Packing £000	Stores £000	Maintenance £000
Indirect labour	98	22	14	11	35	16
Total department overheads						
Apportion maintenance total	-					( )
Apportion stores total	-				( )	
Total production dept overheads						

ITEM 17 (for Task 10)

Journal entry for production overheads

October 20X3

Entries for overhead absorbed during the month

	Debit (£)	Credit (£)
Work in progress: manufacturing dept		
Work in progress: painting and finishing		
Work in progress: packing dept		
Production overhead control		

Entries for overhead under/over absorbed during the month

	Debit (£)	Credit (£)
Overhead over/under absorbed (P+L)		
Production overhead control		

FOULKS LYNCH
PUBLICATIONS

ITEM 18 (for Task 11)

Quality Candles Limited: mail order division
Planned results for December 20X3

	December
Number of cases to be sold	
	£
Candles cost	
Packing materials cost	
Packing labour cost	
Packing overhead cost	
Other overhead cost	
Total costs	
Sales revenue	
Profit	

Space for workings

ITEM 19 (for Task 12 (i))

Quality Candles Limited: mail order division

Planned results for December 20X3: increased activity

	December
Number of cases to be sold	
	£
Candles cost	
Packing materials cost	
Packing labour cost	
Packing overhead cost	
Other overhead cost	
Total costs	
Sales revenue	
Profit	

Space for workings

ITEM 19 (for Task 13 (i))

Working paper for the financial appraisal of purchase of delivery vehicles

Year	Cashflow	Discount factor	Present value
		£ @ 12%	£
20X3	_____	1.000	_____
20X4	_____	0.893	_____
20X5	_____	0.797	_____
20X6	_____	0.712	_____
20X7	_____	0.636	_____

Net present value

Working space for calculation of payback period

FOULKS LYNCH
PUBLICATIONS

PRACTICE SIMULATION 1

COVERAGE OF PERFORMANCE CRITERIA AND RANGE STATEMENTS

Element	PC coverage	Task(s)
6.1	**Record and analyse information relating to direct costs and revenues**	
A	Identify **direct costs** in accordance with the organisation's costing procedures.	1, 2
B	Record and analyse information relating to direct costs.	3, 4, 6
C	Calculate direct costs in accordance with the organisation's policies and procedures.	1, 7
D	Check cost information for **stock** against usage and stock control practices.	3
E	Resolve or refer queries to the appropriate person.	7, 8
6.2	**Record and analyse information relating to the allocation, apportionment and absorption of overhead costs**	
A	Identify **overhead costs** in accordance with the organisation's procedures.	9, 10
B	Attribute overhead costs to production and service cost centres in accordance with agreed **bases of allocation and apportionment**.	9, 10
C	Calculate overhead absorption rates in accordance with agreed **bases of absorption.**	9, 10
D	Record and analyse information relating to overhead costs in accordance with the organisation's procedures.	9, 10
E	Make adjustments for under and over recovered overhead costs in accordance with established procedures.	-
F	Review methods of allocation, apportionment and absorption at regular intervals in discussions with senior staff, and ensure agreed changes to methods are implemented.	-
G	Consult staff working in operational departments to resolve any queries in overhead cost data.	-

6.3	**Prepare and evaluate estimates of costs and revenues**	
A	Identify information relevant to estimating current and future revenues and costs.	11
B	Prepare **estimates** of future income and costs.	-
C	Calculate the effects of variations in capacity on product costs.	-
D	Analyse critical factors affecting costs and revenues using appropriate accounting techniques and draw clear conclusions from the analysis.	11
E	State any assumptions used when evaluating future costs and revenues.	-
F	Identify and evaluate options and solutions for their contribution to organisational goals.	11
G	**Present** recommendations to appropriate people in a clear and concise way and supported by a clear rationale.	-

Any missing range statements should be assessed separately.

THE SITUATION

Your name is Margaret Jones and you work as the cost accountant for Electrotech Ltd, a manufacturer of small electrical products.

Electrotech Ltd has grown through recent times to a size that would now justify more formal techniques for the management and control.

MATERIAL RECORDS

The current practise buying raw materials specifically for individual jobs, has become increasingly unmanageable. There have been several recent incidents where late deliveries of material have led to the workforce being idle and late deliveries of jobs to customers.

A new stock control system is to be introduced.

LABOUR PAYMENT PROCEDURE

Electrotech Ltd has 18 production workers. Payment is at a normal time rate of £5 per hour; overtime, where worked, is at time and a half. The managing director is aware that other similar businesses pay their production workers on a piece-rate basis and is considering this option.

PERSONNEL

The personnel involved in the simulation are as follows:

Managing Director   Robin Smith
Operations Director   Jack Small
Personnel Manager   Toby Stringer

THE TASKS TO BE COMPLETED

PART 1   STOCK CONTROL SYSTEM

TASK 1   The Managing Director, Robin Smith, wishes to introduce a method for valuing issues of material to production. She has heard of the alternative methods, FIFO, LIFO and weighted average but does not understand how they differ. You have produced some sample GRNs and Material Requisitions for illustration purposes

(item 1). Using this information produce sample stores record cards, using the FIFO, LIFO and weighted average methods. (Use the layouts in item 7 to guide you).

TASK 2 Prepare a memo for the Managing Director explaining the differences between the FIFO, LIFO and weighted average methods, referring to the information produced in Task 1 and the memorandum from the Managing Director (item 2).

TASK 3 Write a memorandum to Jack Small, the Operations Director, explaining the main techniques of internal control for the ordering, receipt and issue of raw materials. Include brief descriptions of the documents to be used in such a system and the role they play in the control process.

TASK 4 Information relating to material X103 is given in item 3. This material is used frequently in production and stock control levels are to be introduced to aid the effective management of the material. Calculate the reorder level, maximum and minimum stock levels and the average stock level.

TASK 5 Using the GRNs and material requisitions given (item 1) and the information produced in Task 4 complete the bin card record for material X103 (item 8).

PART 2   LABOUR COSTING SYSTEMS

TASK 6 Refer to the schedule (item 4) showing the work of three production workers over one 4 week period. Calculate figures to show the payments that would be made to these three workers using time based pay and piece-rate with a guaranteed minimum of 80% of time based pay.

TASK 7 The Managing Director wishes to have comparative ideas on how much would be paid to employees if a premium bonus scheme were operated with time-based pay being given plus a bonus of 50% of any time saved. Referring to the information for your answer to Task 8, calculate the figures for time-base pay and piece-rate with minimum guarantee for Charles White, Pamela James and Joanne Peters. Use the form in item 9 to make the comparisons.

TASK 8 Write a memorandum to Toby Stringer, the Personnel Manager, explaining the benefits and disadvantages of payment incentive schemes such as those identified in Tasks 6 and 7. Include in your memo any situations in which such schemes could not or should not be adopted.

PART 3   OVERHEAD ANALYSIS

The company has three productive Cost Centres, Assembly 1, Assembly 2 and packing. Refer to the schedule showing the overhead analysis for the current period (item 5).

TASK 9 Determine the overhead recovery notes for each cost centre and;

TASK 10 Prepare the schedule of production cost of one unit of product '57' and portable mini radio-CD.

The schedules for completion are shown in item 10.

PART 4   INVESTMENT APPRAISAL

The company are considering investing in further delivery vehicles. It will replace the deliveries currently being contracted out. The cost of the vehicle is £25,000 and it has a five year life.

TASK 11 Refer to the schedule of cash flow (item 6) and determine the projects NPV, showing your workings in item 11.

ITEM 1

Sample GRN's and Material Requisitions

Assume that the prices paid for the supplies of X103 from Radiotronics Ltd were £4.50 per unit (GRN No Y504) and £4.60 per unit (GRN Y557).

GOODS RECEIVED NOTE (GRN)	
Date: *8 Jan* GRN No: *Y 504*	
Item	**Qty**
X103 Capacitors	400

Supplier: *Radiotronics*

Quality checked: *John White*

Received by: Ben B

Storeskeeper: Ben B   **Bin card** **entered**...........

GOODS RECEIVED NOTE (GRN)	
Date: *20 Jan* GRN No: *Y 557*	
Item	**Qty**
X103 Capacitors	320

Supplier: *Radiotronics*

Quality checked: *JW*

Received by: Ben B

Storeskeeper: Ben B   **Bin card** **entered**...........

MATERIAL REQUISITION		
Dept: *Production* Serial no: *22450*		
Date: *8 Jan*		
Code no.	**Description**	**Qty**
X103	*S/L Capacitors*	180

Authorised by: *KK*   **Received by:** *JH*

Storeskeeper: Ben B   **Bin card entered**

MATERIAL REQUISITION		
Dept: *Production* Serial no: *22568*		
Date: *12 Jan*		
Code no.	**Description**	**Qty**
X103	*Seamed Leaden Capacitors*	180

Authorised by: *KK*   **Received by:** *JH*

Storeskeeper: Ben B   **Bin card entered**

MATERIAL REQUISITION		
Dept: *Production* Serial no: *22691*		
Date: *21 Jan*		
Code no.	**Description**	**Qty**
X103	*S/L Capacitors*	220

Authorised by: *KK*   **Received by:** *KM*

Storeskeeper: Ben B   **Bin card entered**

MATERIAL REQUISITION		
Dept: *Production* Serial no: *22742*		
Date: *25 Jan*		
Code no.	**Description**	**Qty**
X103	*Seamed Leaden Capacitors*	140

Authorised by: *KK*   **Received by:** *Jim Black*

Storeskeeper: Ben B **Bin card entered**

FOULKS LYNCH
PUBLICATIONS

	Costs Centres	Overhead Analysis	
	Assembly 1	Assembly 2	Packing
Overhead allocated	50,000	40,000	35,000
Overhead apportioned	15,500	10,500	12,500
	£65,500	£50,500	£47,500
Direct labour hours	8,500	8,000	7,500

ITEM 2

MEMORANDUM

To: Cost Accountant

From: Managing Director

Date:

Subject: **Stock Issue Pricing**

I have come across some statements regarding stock issue pricing and would be grateful if you could include answers to these in your report. They are as follows:

1   LIFO follows (typical) physical stock distribution.

2   SSAP 9 would tend to support FIFO.

3   Weighted average is capable of providing the most up-to-date and appropriate product costings for determining and setting product selling prices.

4   In times of inflation LIFO produces lower balance sheet stock valuations.

5   In times of inflation FIFO produces lower period profit figures.

ITEM 3

Material X103 (Estimate)

Usage in production: 9,840 units

Daily usage: Variable – between 30 and 50 units per working day

Supplier delivery times: variable – between 6 and 8 working days

Re-order quantity: 1,000 units

Assume 240 working days.

ITEM 4

The work of three production workers over one 4 week period is as follows:

Employee:	Charles White	Pamela James	Joanne Peters
Hours worked:	172.0	168.0	180.0
Product output:	60 units	50 units	52 units
Standard hours per product:	3	3.5	2.8
Piecerate:	£14	£16	£12.50

Standard working week = 40 hours

Normal time rate = £5 per hour

Overtime is paid at time and half.

ITEM 5

Details of one month's payroll figures for Electrotech Ltd appear below:

Detail	Amount
Total gross wage costs (Payroll records) (Gross for employees before deductions of £11,000 for tax & NI)	£42,000
Employers NI	£2,500
Total	**£44,500**
Breakdown	
Direct worker costs (incl. employers NI)	£28,400
Overtime premium (direct workers)	£2,300
Unavoidable idle time	£2,000
Avoidable idle time	£1,500
Administrative staff costs	£8,000
Selling & distribution staff costs	£2,300
Total	**£44,500**

FOULKS LYNCH
PUBLICATIONS

ITEM 6

CAPITAL INVESTMENT

Special delivery vehicle capital cost £25,000. Project's useful life 5 years.

Cash flows from the project (savings on current contract)

YR	1	£7,000
	2	£8,000
	3	£9,000
	4	£7,500
	5	£7,500

Cost of capital 15%.

ANSWER TABLES

ITEM 7 (for Task 1)

MATERIAL X103 – STORES LEDGER - FIFO								
Date	**Materials received**			**Materials issued**			**Materials stock**		
	Qty	Unit (£)	Value (£)	Qty	Unit (£)	Value (£)	Qty	Unit (£)	Value (£)
1 January							200	4.40	880

MATERIAL X103 – STORES LEDGER - LIFO								
Date	**Materials received**			**Materials issued**			**Materials stock**		
	Qty	Unit (£)	Value (£)	Qty	Unit (£)	Value (£)	Qty	Unit (£)	Value (£)
1 January							220	4.40	880

MATERIAL X103 – STORES LEDGER – WEIGHTED AVERAGE								
Date	**Materials received**			**Materials issued**			**Materials stock**		
	Qty	Unit (£)	Value (£)	Qty	Unit (£)	Value (£)	Qty	Unit (£)	Value (£)
1 January							200	4.40	880

FOULKS LYNCH
PUBLICATIONS

ITEM 8 (for Task 5)

STORES LEDGER/BIN CARD									
Materials Code			ROL				Minimum S/L		
Item description			ROQ				Maximum S/L		

Receipts			Issues			On order			
Date	GRN Ref	Quantity	Date	Req'n Ref	Quantity	Physical balance	Date	Ref	Quantity
1 Jan						200	31 Dec	I210	400

ITEM 10 (for Task 10)

Production Cost Schedule '57' mini radio-CD player

Direct labour

      4.5 hours × £5 per hour

Direct materials

      3 units × £4.50

      2 units × £2.50

Production overhead

Assembly 1	2 hours × £
Assembly 2	2.25 hours × £
Packing	0.25 hours × £
	£

ITEM 11 (for Task 10)

Cash flow	Year 1	2	3	4	5
£(25,000)	£7,000	£8,000	£9,000	£7,500	£7,500
NPV factor 1.00	0.870	0.757	0.658	0.573	0.498
NPV					

Net Present Value   £

FOULKS LYNCH
PUBLICATIONS

PRACTICE SIMULATION 2

COVERAGE OF PERFORMANCE CRITERIA AND RANGE STATEMENTS

Element	PC coverage	Task(s)
6.1	**Record and analyse information relating to direct costs and revenues**	
A	Identify **direct costs** in accordance with the organisation's costing procedures.	1
B	Record and analyse information relating to direct costs.	6
C	Calculate direct costs in accordance with the organisation's policies and procedures.	4
D	Check cost information for **stock** against usage and stock control practices.	-
E	Resolve or refer queries to the appropriate person.	6
6.2	**Record and analyse information relating to the allocation, apportionment and absorption of overhead costs**	
A	Identify **overhead costs** in accordance with the organisation's procedures.	1, 2, 7
B	Attribute overhead costs to production and service cost centres in accordance with agreed **bases of allocation and apportionment**.	3
C	Calculate overhead absorption rates in accordance with agreed **bases of absorption.**	3
D	Record and analyse information relating to overhead costs in accordance with the organisation's procedures.	2, 3, 4
E	Make adjustments for under and over recovered overhead costs in accordance with established procedures.	5
F	Review methods of allocation, apportionment and absorption at regular intervals in discussions with senior staff, and ensure agreed changes to methods are implemented.	1
G	Consult staff working in operational departments to resolve any queries in overhead cost data.	-

6.3	**Prepare and evaluate estimates of costs and revenues**	
A	Identify information relevant to estimating current and future revenues and costs.	8
B	Prepare **estimates** of future income and costs.	8
C	Calculate the effects of variations in capacity on product costs.	2
D	Analyse critical factors affecting costs and revenues using appropriate accounting techniques and draw clear conclusions from the analysis.	8
E	State any assumptions used when evaluating future costs and revenues.	-
F	Identify and evaluate options and solutions for their contribution to organisational goals.	8
G	**Present** recommendations to appropriate people in a clear and concise way and supported by a clear rationale.	-

Any missing range statements should be assessed separately.

THE SITUATION

Your name is Joseph Ballestrini and you work as the cost accountant for Smorlek Ltd, a manufacturer of small electrical products.

The Managing Director has recently been appointed to the post from a background in personnel and human resources and is keen to gain an understanding of costing systems and related terminology.

Anticipated overhead cost detail is being collated to enable the company to fully calculate expected product costs for 200X. Currently labour hours are used as a basis for setting overhead absorption rates (OARs).

The company has two production cost centres, Assembly and Finishing and Packaging. You are considering changing to machine hours as a basis for setting the OAR in the Assembly department. Labour hours will continue to be used as the basis for setting OARs in the Finishing and Packaging departments.

There are two service cost centres, Canteen and Repairs.

THE TASKS TO BE PERFORMED

PART 1   COST CLASSIFICATION

TASK 1   Refer to the memorandum (item 1). Draft a suitable reply.

TASK 2   Information relating to electricity power costs over the final six months of 200W is given in item 2. Use the high-low method to estimate fixed and variable power costs generally are expected to rise by 6%. Present your calculations on the pro-forma (item 6).

PART 2   OVERHEAD ABSORPTION

TASK 3   Data relating to forecast overhead costs for 200X is given (item 3), together with additional information to be used for apportioning overhead costs to cost centres. Using this information calculate overhead absorption rates for the Assembly department and the Finishing and Packaging department. Present your answer as laid out in item 8.

TASK 4   Using your answer to Task 5 complete the production cost schedule (item 7).

TASK 5   Refer to the memorandum for the Managing Director (item 4) and your answer to Task 3. Draft a suitable reply using a memorandum and use the working sheets (item 9).

PART 3   LABOUR ANALYSIS

TASK 6   Information relating to labour turnover is given (item 5). Referring to this information, calculate labour turnover for the two years, 200V and 200W, for both production and non-production workers. Indicate any reservations that you may have about the figures and what other information you would like if the figures were to be of any real use. Use the blank form (item 11) for your calculations and comments.

PART 4   DIRECT EXPENSES

TASK 7   The Managing Director is concerned about the level of depreciation that is charged to the production departments and the method by which this is calculated. Write a memorandum to him explaining the purpose of depreciation and the main methods of depreciation available to a manufacturing concern.

PART 5   MARGINAL COST ANALYSIS

TASK 8   The Company intend to introduce a new product 'X7' CD player.

The proposed selling price is £70 per unit and the variable cost per unit is estimated as £30.

Fixed costs apportioned to the activities involved with the manufacture of this production are £65,000.

Planned production 5,000 units.

Using this information and the schedule shown in item 10, determine the break even point in units of this product and calculate the margin of safety in units of output.

ITEM 1

MEMORANDUM

To: Cost Accountant

From: Managing Director

Date: 31 January 200X

Subject: Cost accounting terminology

I realise from reading some of your reports that I am not totally clear regarding the detailed meaning of some cost accounting terminology. The terms that have caused some confusion are the following:

- direct and indirect costs

- variable and fixed costs

- are all variable costs direct and all fixed costs indirect?

- overheads

- allocation, apportionment and absorption

- semi fixed and semi variable costs.

Please could you send me a memorandum explaining these areas to me for future reference.

ITEM 2

	Power costs £	Machine hours of activity in production
July 200W	23,100	300
August 200W	26,650	360
September 200W	21,400	280
October 200W	27,150	380
November 200W	29,200	410
December 200W	25,200	340

Supervisor's overtime of £1,000 was included in the budget. Due to efficient production scheduling only £400 was spent.

ITEM 3

FORECAST OVERHEAD COSTS FOR 200X

Overhead expenditure item	Anticipated expense
Rent for premises	£24,000
Rates	£4,800
Insurances	£3,500
Power costs (based on 3,880 total machine hours: 3,600 machine hrs for Assembly, the remainder for Finishing & packaging)	£29,552
Heating & lighting	£3,800
Canteen supplies	£1,250
Depreciation: Assembly	£3,400
Finishing & packaging	£1,050
Production supervisor (Salary)	£12,000
Allocated costs - Repairs	£5,600
Other allocated costs: Assembly	£8,600
Finishing & packaging	£2,100

The company will use floor space to apportion rent, rates, and heating & lighting costs. Employee numbers will be used to apportion canteen costs and costs of supervision. Machine hours will be used to apportion repairs costs - relevant machine hours being simply those for Assembly and Finishing & packaging. Insurance costs are to be split 55:35:5:5 across Assembly, Finishing & packaging, Canteen and Repairs, respectively.

Power costs are to be split simply between the two production departments on the basis of machine hours.

Further details are as follows:

	Assembly	Finishing & packaging	Canteen	Repairs
Floor area (sq mtrs)	350	70	15	15
Employees	16	2	1	1

Expected labour hours in Finishing & packaging for 200X total 3,680.

ITEM 4

MEMORANDUM

To: Cost Accountant

From: Managing Director

Date: 31 January 200X

Subject: Under/over absorption of overheads.

I do not understand what under/over absorption is or why it occurs. If, for example, actual costs and activity levels in 200X were to be:

Actual overhead cost:	Assembly	£82,600
	Finishing and Packaging	£15,540
Activity levels:	Assembly machine hours	£3,350
	Finishing and Packaging labour hours	£3,700

Would there be any over/under absorption in each department?

Please would you:

- produce a sample calculation based on the above figures for each department

- illustrate how the over/under absorption is entered into the cost accounts

- provide a brief explanation of your workings

I also do not understand why we cannot use actual overheads to calculate product cost. Surely this would avoid all of the problems of over/under absorption and make your job much easier. Please explain why pre-set overhead absorption rates are used.

Finally, I am concerned that the under/over absorption will distort the product costs and the overall profit and loss that the business shows. Is this so?

ITEM 5

LABOUR TURNOVER

		Production workers	Non-production workers
Average number of employees	200V	8	5
	200W	15	8
Number of leavers during the year	200V	0	2
	200W	5	4

ANSWER TABLES

ITEM 6 (for Task 2)

	Machine hours of activity in production	Power costs £
High activity:		
Low activity:	_____	_____
Difference:		
Variable cost per machine hour:		
Estimate of fixed costs:		
Projections for 200X: Fixed costs (total):		
Variable cost per machine hour:		

ITEM 7 (for Task 4)

Overhead allocation and apportionment schedule						
Overhead	Basis	Assembly £	Finishing & packaging £	Canteen £	Repairs £	Total £
Budget overhead		____	____	____	____	____
Reapportionment of service costs						
Canteen						
Repairs						
		____	____	____	____	____
Budgeted production overhead						
		____	____	____	____	____
OARs						
Assembly						
Finishing & packaging						

ITEM 8 (for Task 5)

PRODUCTION COST SCHEDULE - 200X - SW Radio		
		£
Costs: Labour		8.00
Materials		6.50
Overhead: Assembly		
Finishing & packaging		
		____
		____

Machine hrs: 0.5 (0.25 in Assembly)

Labour hours in Finishing & packaging - 0.75

ITEM 9 (for Task 7)

Working Sheets

Over/under absorption of overheads	
Assembly	
	£
Finishing & packaging	
	£

Production overhead control account - assembly

	£		£

Production overhead control account - finishing and packaging

	£		£

ITEM 10 (for Task 8)

New Product 'X7' CD Player

£ (per unit)

Selling price

Variable cost

———

Contribution

———

Break even point in units

=

———

=   ——— Units

Margin of safety
= 5,000 units   _____ break-even
point in units

ITEM 11 (for Task 9)

	Production workers	Non-production workers
Labour turnover		
200V		
200W		
Comment:		

FOULKS LYNCH
PUBLICATIONS

PRACTICE SIMULATION 3

COVERAGE OF PERFORMANCE CRITERIA AND RANGE STATEMENTS

Element	PC coverage	Task(s)
6.1	**Record and analyse information relating to direct costs and revenues**	
A	Identify **direct costs** in accordance with the organisation's costing procedures.	1
B	Record and analyse information relating to direct costs.	1, 3
C	Calculate direct costs in accordance with the organisation's policies and procedures.	3
D	Check cost information for **stock** against usage and stock control practices.	2
E	Resolve or refer queries to the appropriate person.	4
6.2	**Record and analyse information relating to the allocation, apportionment and absorption of overhead costs**	
A	Identify **overhead costs** in accordance with the organisation's procedures.	5, 6, 7
B	Attribute overhead costs to production and service cost centres in accordance with agreed **bases of allocation and apportionment**.	6
C	Calculate overhead absorption rates in accordance with agreed **bases of absorption**.	5, 6
D	Record and analyse information relating to overhead costs in accordance with the organisation's procedures.	6
E	Make adjustments for under and over recovered overhead costs in accordance with established procedures.	7
F	Review methods of allocation, apportionment and absorption at regular intervals in discussions with senior staff, and ensure agreed changes to methods are implemented.	5
G	Consult staff working in operational departments to resolve any queries in overhead cost data.	-

6.3	Prepare and evaluate estimates of costs and revenues	
A	Identify information relevant to estimating current and future revenues and costs.	9
B	Prepare **estimates** of future income and costs.	9
C	Calculate the effects of variations in capacity on product costs.	9
D	Analyse critical factors affecting costs and revenues using appropriate accounting techniques and draw clear conclusions from the analysis.	8, 9
E	State any assumptions used when evaluating future costs and revenues.	-
F	Identify and evaluate options and solutions for their contribution to organisational goals.	8
G	**Present** recommendations to appropriate people in a clear and concise way and supported by a clear rationale.	8

Any missing range statements should be assessed separately.

THE SITUATION

INTRODUCTION

Your name is Tracy Green and you work as an accounts assistant for Growmore Limited, a manufacturer of specialist garden equipment.

COST CENTRES

The production cost centres in Growmore Limited are a machining department, an assembly department and a packing department.

- Work in the assembly department and packing department is labour-intensive

- Work in the machining department is machine-intensive and the machines are operated by a number of direct employees

In addition to the production cost centres there is also a stores department and a canteen.

Cost accounting records

Growmore Limited uses the LIFO method for valuing issues of materials to production and stocks of materials.

The company is registered for VAT and all of its outputs are standard-rated. This means that VAT on its purchases can always be reclaimed and should therefore be ignored in the cost records.

The accounts code list for the company includes the following codes:

Cost centre codes		*Expenditure codes*	
10	Machining department	05	Direct materials
20	Finishing department	06	Indirect materials
30	Packaging department	07	Direct wages
40	Stores	08	Indirect wages
50	Canteen	09	Indirect revenue expenses
		10	Depreciation production equipment

The company uses labour hours to absorb overhead in the assembly department, machine hours to absorb overhead in the machining department and a unit basis to absorb overhead in the packing department. The company operates a standard costing system and all of the cost ledger transactions are made at standard cost.

PERSONNEL

The personnel involved in the simulation are as follows:

Production manager   Amy Rowel

General manager   Stuart York

In the simulation you will begin by dealing with certain transactions in the month of March 2002, and you will then be involved in forecasting outcomes for the company's financial year ending 31 March 2003. Finally, you will use your results to account for transactions in July 2002. Note that for many of the tasks you will need to prepare rough workings; you should use the paper provided for this purpose.

THE TASKS TO BE COMPELTED

PART 1   TRANSACTIONS IN MARCH 2002

TASK 1   Refer to the purchase invoices and materials requisitions (items 1 & 2). Using this information you are required to complete the stores records card (item 8) for the month of March 2002. You are reminded that the company uses the LIFO method. You may assume that suppliers raise invoices on the same day as goods are delivered.

TASK 2   The General Manager has noticed that orders for larger quantities of timber attract a higher trade discount. Referring to the information given (item 3) relating to timber purchase and stock holding cost calculate the economic order quantity using the pro-forma (item 9). Write a brief memo to the General Manager explaining your recommendation.

TASK 3   Timesheets for two employees of Growmore Limited are shown (item 10). Using the information contained in the internal policy documents (item 4), you are required to analyse their wages for the week ending 6 March 2002, as follows:

- Complete the total column in each timesheet.

- Calculate the bonus earned by each employee on each day and in total for the week, and enter the appropriate amounts on the timesheets.

- Complete the analysis at the bottom of each timesheet.

- Enter the appropriate figures on the cost ledger data entry sheet (item 11).

TASK 4   The General Manager is considering replacing the current individual bonus scheme, which has been in operation for several years, with a group bonus scheme. Explain the advantages and disadvantages of a group bonus scheme by writing a memo. Date your memo 10 March 2002.

PART 2   OVERHEAD ABSORPTION FOR 2002/03

TASK 5   Refer to the memo from the General Manager (item 5). Using a memo, explain the reasons for using different bases to absorb overhead in each production department.

TASK 6   Refer to the information given in item 6. Using this information, you are required to calculate 2002/03 overhead absorption rates for each production department: assembly (labour hour rate), machining (machine hour rate) and packing (unit rate). Use the analysis sheet (item 12).

TASK 7 Using the overhead absorption rate that you calculated in Task 6 and the information in item 6, calculate the production overhead absorbed in the Assembly department during the quarter ending 30 June 2002. Insert your result in the working sheet (item 13).

Calculate the amount to be transferred to the profit and loss account for the quarter ending 30 June 2002, in respect of under or over absorbed production overheads for the Assembly department. Indicate clearly whether the overheads are under or over absorbed for the quarter.

PART 3   INVESTMENT APPRAISAL

TASK 8 Refer to the memo (item 7). Reply to the request from Stuart York the General Manager regarding the proposed investment. The blank schedule for your reply is item 14.

PART 4   MARGINAL COST ANALYSIS

TASK 9 The new equipment referred to in Part 3 will be used in the development of a new product coded 'XX125' which will have a selling price of £90. The variable cost per unit is £50 and the relevant fixed costs linked to this production are £75,000.

Planned output is 6,000 units. Using this information and the schedule shown in item 15 determine the break-even point in units of output and the margin of safety as a % of planned output.

ITEM 1 – SALES INVOICES

<table>
<tr><td colspan="6" align="center">**SALES INVOICE**</td></tr>
<tr><td colspan="3">**FOREST SUPPLIES LIMITED**
Old Forest
Southampton
SO9 4JX
Telephone: 01792 563421</td><td colspan="3">VAT registration: 391 7284 97

Date/tax point: 4 March 2002</td></tr>
<tr><td colspan="3">**Invoice to:**
Growmore Ltd
22 North Road
Ipswich
IS3 92D</td><td colspan="3">Invoice number: 469X

Your order: 234</td></tr>
<tr><td>**Item description**</td><td>**Quantity**</td><td>**Unit price**

£</td><td>**Trade Discount @ 20%**
£</td><td>**Net price**

£</td><td>**Total**

£</td></tr>
<tr><td>Timber (10 metre lengths)</td><td>200</td><td>22.50</td><td>4.50</td><td>18.00</td><td>3,600.00</td></tr>
<tr><td colspan="5">Total
VAT at 17.5%</td><td>3,600.00
630.00</td></tr>
<tr><td colspan="5">Total due</td><td>4,230.00</td></tr>
<tr><td colspan="5">Terms: net 30 days</td><td></td></tr>
</table>

 FOULKS LYNCH PUBLICATIONS

SALES INVOICE

FOREST SUPPLIES LIMITED
Old Forest
Southampton
SO9 4JX
Telephone: 01792 563421

VAT registration: 391 7284 97

Date/tax point: 11 March 2002

Invoice to:
Growmore Ltd
22 North Road
Ipswich
IS3 92D

Invoice number: 504X

Your order: 237

Item description	Quantity	Unit price £	Trade Discount @ 30% £	Net price £	Total £
Timber (10 metre lengths)	500 boxes	22.50	6.75	15.75	7,875.00
Total VAT at 17.5%					7,875.00 1,378.13
Total due					9,253.13
Terms: net 30 days					

SALES INVOICE

FOREST SUPPLIES LIMITED
Old Forest
Southampton
SO9 4JX
Telephone: 01792 563421

VAT registration: 391 7284 97

Date/tax point: 18 March 2002

Invoice to:
*Growmore Ltd
22 North Road
Ipswich
IS3 92D*

Invoice number: 526X

Your order: 245

Item description	Quantity	Unit price £	Trade Discount @ 10% £	Net price £	Total £
Timber (10 metre lengths)	100	22.50	2.25	20.25	2,025.00
Total					2,025.00
VAT at 17.5%					354.38
Total due					2,379.38
Terms: net 30 days					

ITEM 2 – MATERIALS REQUISITIONS

<table>
<tr><td colspan="3">MATERIALS REQUISITION</td></tr>
<tr><td colspan="2">DATE   8 March 2002</td><td>NUMBER   2731</td></tr>
<tr><td colspan="3">DEPARTMENT   Machining</td></tr>
<tr><td>QUANTITY</td><td>CODE</td><td>DESCRIPTION</td></tr>
<tr><td>150</td><td>T10</td><td>Timber (10 metre lengths)</td></tr>
<tr><td colspan="3">SIGNATURE   Amy Rowel</td></tr>
</table>

<table>
<tr><td colspan="3">MATERIALS REQUISITION</td></tr>
<tr><td colspan="2">DATE   13 March 2002</td><td>NUMBER   2738</td></tr>
<tr><td colspan="3">DEPARTMENT   Machining</td></tr>
<tr><td>QUANTITY</td><td>CODE</td><td>DESCRIPTION</td></tr>
<tr><td>350</td><td>T10</td><td>Timber (10 metre lengths)</td></tr>
<tr><td colspan="3">SIGNATURE   Amy Rowel</td></tr>
</table>

<table>
<tr><td colspan="3">MATERIALS REQUISITION</td></tr>
<tr><td colspan="2">DATE   15 March 2002</td><td>NUMBER   2745</td></tr>
<tr><td colspan="3">DEPARTMENT   Machining</td></tr>
<tr><td>QUANTITY</td><td>CODE</td><td>DESCRIPTION</td></tr>
<tr><td>225</td><td>T10</td><td>Timber (10 metre lengths)</td></tr>
<tr><td colspan="3">SIGNATURE   Amy Rowel</td></tr>
</table>

MATERIALS REQUISITION		
DATE **22 March 2002**		NUMBER **2747**
DEPARTMENT **Machining**		
QUANTITY	CODE	DESCRIPTION
80	**T10**	**Timber (10 metre lengths)**
SIGNATURE **Amy Rowel**		

FOREST SUPPLIES PRICE LIST 2002	
	£
Timber (10 metre lengths)	22.50

The following trade discounts apply to Growmore Ltd;

Order Size	Trade Discount
1 –199	10%
200 – 399	20%
400 and above	30%

ITEM 3

INFORMATION RELATING TO ORDERING AND STOCKHOLDING COSTS

Order costs are estimated to be £20 per order for all orders placed.

Storage cost of one metre length of timber is estimated to be £10.50 for a year. Over a year, the average number of lengths in storage is half the order quantity. So for an order size, x, the storage cost will be:

Average stock level x £10.50 = $£\dfrac{x}{2} \times 10.50$

The annual demand for timber (10 metre lengths) is estimated to be 10,000 lengths. So for an order size of 500, for example, 20 orders would be place during the year ($\dfrac{10,000}{500}$)

ITEM 4 – INTERNAL POLICY DOCUMENTS

INTERNAL POLICY DOCUMENT

Document no. 15

Subject: **Wages**

Issued: **December 2001**

DIRECT LABOUR RATES TO BE PAID

Employee grade	£ per hour
1	8.00
2	6.50
3	5.00

The above rates are also payable for any hours spent on indirect work.

Direct employees work an eight hour day.

Overtime (any hours worked in excess of eight per day): employees are to be paid for one and a half hours for every hour of overtime that they work.

Employees bonus is the subject of a separate policy document (number 16).

Employees are to be credited with eight hours for any full days when they are sick, on holiday, or engaged in training activities. Half or part days are credited on a pro rata basis. These hours are to be paid at the basic rate.

ANALYSIS OF WAGES

The following are to be treated as direct labour costs:

   *Payment for hours spent on direct tasks

   *The basic pay for overtime spent on direct tasks

The following are to be treated as indirect labour costs:

   *Overtime premium payments

   *Bonus payments

   *Idle time payments

   *Holiday pay, sick pay and training pay

INTERNAL POLICY DOCUMENT

Document no. 16

Subject: **Bonus Payments**

Issued: **January 1999**

Bonus is payable on the basis of the formula: $\dfrac{(\text{Time allowed} - \text{time taken}) \times \text{hourly rate}}{2}$

2 units produced in any single day.

Time allowed per unit is

         9 minutes for Assembly

         10 minutes for Machining

ITEM 5

To: Tracy Green

From: Stuart York

Date: 30 March 2002

Subject: Overhead Absorption

I am reviewing the current system of allocating overhead to products and am concerned that the current method of using a different basis in each production department is too complicated and unnecessary. Can you give me your views on this issue?

ITEM 6

PRODUCTION OVERHEADS FOR THE YEAR TO 31 MARCH 2003

Growmore Limited rents its production premises. The rent and rates for the year to 31 March 2003 will amount to £125,000.

There is a canteen for production staff and the costs are estimated to be £32,000.

Specialist machinery and equipment owned by Growmore is subject to a maintenance contract covering preventive and urgent maintenance, parts, labour and call out charges. For the year to 31 March 2003 the maintenance company will charge £60,000 in respect of the machinery in the machining department. Depreciation is on a straight line basis with the machines having an estimated life of 5 years.

The production manager's salary will be £30,000 for the year; he divides his time about equally between the three production departments. The storekeeper's salary will be £20,000 and the canteen staff earn £18,000 in total.

Other production overheads for the year are estimated at £60,000. The general manager has suggested this should be divided evenly across the three production departments.

The following data is also available:

	Assembly	Machining	Packing	Stores	Canteen
Floor area (sq metres)	2,500	1,750	1,250	575	425
Number of employees	75	21	37	3	2
Cost of machinery	£11,500	£785,000	£25,400	£8,500	4,250
Direct labour hours	120,000	31,500	55,500		
Machine hours	10,000	80,000	15,400		
Number of materials requisitions	31,175	27,675	24,100		

The total number of production units is forecast to be £450,000.

ASSEMBLY DEPARTMENT

Actual Results for Quarter Ending 30 June 2002

Actual direct labour hours	32,500
Actual machine hours	2,200
Actual overhead incurred	£33,250

ITEM 7

MEMO

To: Tracy Green

From: Stuart York

RE: Investment in new machine

You are aware that we plan to expand capacity by purchasing a new cutting machine.

The initial cost is £75,000 and the cash flows from incremental business will be – over a five year period:

YR	1	£30,000
	2	£40,000
	3	£25,000
	4	£20,000
	5	£20,000

Our current cost of capital is 15%.

Could you please prepare an evaluation of the proposed investment using both the payback and NPV methods of appraisal.

FOULKS LYNCH
PUBLICATIONS

ANSWER TABLES

ITEM 8 (for Task 1)

STORES LEDGER ACCOUNT

Material description: Timber (10 metre lengths)

Code No: T10

Date	Receipts			Issues			Stock balance		
	Quantity	Price £ per length	Total £	Quantity	Price £ per length	Total £	Quantity	Price £ per length	Total £
1 March							50	17.50	875.50

ITEM 9 (for Task 2)

APPENDIX TO MEMORANDUM

Order Size	Number of orders placed during year	Ordering cost £	Storage cost £	Purchase cost £	Price £ per length	Total Cost £	Purchase Cost £
100							
200							
300							
400							
500							
600							
700							
800							

ITEM 10 (for Task 3)

Timesheet	Week ending		6 March 2002			

Employee name	Jim Davis		Employee number		56	

Department	Assembly		Employee grade		2	

Activity	**Monday**	**Tuesday**	**Wednesday**	**Thursday**	**Friday**	**Total**
	Hours	Hours	Hours	Hours	Hours	Hours
Assembly	7	10	4		4	
Holiday			4	8		
Waiting for work	1					
Training					4	
Total hours payable	8	10	8	8	8	
Number of units produced	65	72	30	0	32	

Standard time for units produced
Time taken
Time saved

Bonus payable

Signed	Jim Davis			Manager	Amy Rowel	

Analysis for week	*Hours*	*Rate per hour £*	*Wages cost £*
Direct wages			
Indirect wages			
Basic hours			
Overtime premium			
Bonus			
	_____	_____	_____
	_____	_____	_____

Timesheet   Week ending   6 March 2002

Employee name   Ron O'Sullivan   Employee number   23

Department   Machining   Employee grade   1

Activity	**Monday** Hours	**Tuesday** Hours	**Wednesday** Hours	**Thursday** Hours	**Friday** Hours	**Total** Hours
Machining	10	6	6		8	
Waiting for work		2	2			
Sick				8		
Training					2	
Total hours payable for	10	8	8	8	10	
Number of units produced	70	51	62	0	62	

Standard time for units
produced
Time taken
Time saved

Bonus payable

Signed   Ron O'Sullivan   Manager   Amy Rowel

Analysis for week		*Hours*	*Rate per hour* £	*Wages cost* £
Direct wages				
Indirect wages				
Basic hours				
Overtime premium				
Bonus				
		———	———	———
		———	———	———

ITEM 11 (for Task 3)

COST LEDGER DATA ENTRY SHEET

Week ending _____

Debit accounts

	Cost centre Code	Expenditure code	Amount to be debited £
	C10	07	
	C20	07	
	C30	07	
	C40	07	
	C50	07	
	C10	08	
	C20	08	
	C30	08	
	C40	08	
	C50	08	

Check total: total wages for the two employees

ITEM 12 (for Task 6)

OVERHEAD ANALYSIS SHEET: 2002/03

Overhead expense:	Basis of allocation/ apportionment	Total £	Assembly Dept £	Machining Dept £	Packing Dept £	Stores £	Canteen £
Total							
Re-apportion canteen							
Total							

Re-apportion stores

Total production cost centre
overhead

Direct labour

Machine hours

Production units 2002/03

ITEM 13 (for Task 7)

Working sheet for calculation of overhead under/over
absorbed

Assembly department, quarter ending 30 June 2002

Production overhead absorbed   £

Actual production overhead incurred   £

Production overhead under or over absorbed,   £
to be transferred to profit and loss account

ITEM 14 (for Task 8)

INVESTMENT APPRAISAL – NEW CUTTING MACHINE

Payback period

		Cash flow	*Cumulative*
Yr	1		
	2		
	3		
	4		
	5		

payback period
=

NPV Schedule   *(15% Discount Rate)*

		(Outflow)	*Inflow*	*NPV factor*	*NPV*
Yr	0	(75,000)		1.0	
	1			0.870	
	2			0.757	
	3			0.658	
	4			0.573	
	5			0.498	
				NPV	

ITEM 15 (for Task 9)

MARGINAL COST ANALYSIS – NEW PRODUCT LINE CODE 'XX125'

	£
Selling price per unit	_____
Variable cost per unit	_____
Contribution per unit	_____

Break-even point in units

=   _____

=   _____   units

Margin of safety in units

planned output – breakeven point in units

=   _____   units

% of planned output   =   _____   %

FOULKS LYNCH
PUBLICATIONS

SPECIMEN EXAMINATION

This examination paper is in TWO sections.

You have to show competence in BOTH sections.

You should therefore attempt and aim to complete EVERY task in BOTH sections.

Blank space for workings is available on pages and but all essential workings should be included within your answers, where appropriate.

You should spend about 90 minutes on each section.

Both sections are based on Gift Ltd.

DATA

Gift Ltd manufactures and sells toys. You work as an accounting technician at Gift Ltd, reporting to the Finance Director.

All toys are manufactured using plastic. The biggest selling item is Meg, a toy doll made from pink plastic. The company operates an integrated absorption costing system. Stocks are valued on a first in first out basis.

The Finance Director has given you the following tasks:

TASK 1.1

Complete the following stock card for pink plastic using the FIFO method for valuing issues to production and stocks of materials.

STOCK CARD

Product: Pink plastic

	Receipts			Issues			Balance	
Date	Quantity kgs	Cost per kg £	Total cost £	Quantity kgs	Cost per kg £	Total cost £	Quantity kgs	Total cost £
							10,000	10,000
b/f 1.11.03								
6.11.03	20,000	1.10	22,000				30,000	32,000
11.11.03				16,000				
17.11.03	10,000	1.20	12,000					
19.11.03				20,000				

ADDITIONAL DATA

All issues of pink plastic are for the manufacture of Meg dolls. The following cost accounting codes are used to record material costs:

Code number	Description
1000	Stock of pink plastic
1100	Work in progress - Meg dolls
3000	Creditors control

TASK 1.2

Complete the table below to record separately the two purchases and two issues of pink plastic in the cost accounting records.

Date	Code	Dr	Cr
6 Nov	1000		
6 Nov	3000		
11 Nov	1000		
11 Nov	1100		
17 Nov	1000		
17 Nov	3000		
19 Nov	1000		
19 Nov	1100		

ADDITIONAL DATA

Direct labour overtime payments are included in direct costs. The following data relates to the production of Meg dolls for November:

Total direct labour hours worked	12,000 hours
Normal time hours	10,600 hours
Overtime hours	1,400 hours
Normal time rate per hour	£6 per hour
Overtime premium per hour	£3 per hour

TASK 1.3

Calculate the total cost of direct labour for November.

ADDITIONAL DATA

Gift Ltd has the following departments:

- Warehouse
- Manufacturing
- Sales
- Accounting

The budgeted and actual fixed overheads of the company for November were as follows:

	£
Depreciation	7,400
Rent	2,500
Other property overheads	3,200
Accounting overheads	6,250
Staff costs:	
Warehouse	4,230
Indirect manufacturing	3,015
Sales	6,520
Accounting	5,160
Total budgeted and actual fixed overheads	38,275

The following information is also relevant:

Department	% of floor space occupied	Net book value of fixed assets
		£000
Warehouse	15%	180
Manufacturing	70%	540
Sales	10%	-
Accounting	5%	80
	100%	800

Overheads are allocated and apportioned between departments using the most appropriate basis.

TASK 1.4

Complete the following table showing the allocation and apportionment of fixed overheads between the four departments.

Fixed overheads for November	Basis	Total £	Warehouse £	Manufacturing £	Sales £	Accounting £
Depreciation		7,400				
Rent		2,500				
Other property overheads		3,200				
Accounting overheads		6,250				
Staff costs		18,925				
		38,275				

ADDITIONAL DATA

Manufacturing fixed overheads are absorbed on the basis of budgeted direct labour hours.

The following information relates to the manufacturing department for November:

- The budgeted number of direct labour hours was 20,000 hours.

- The actual direct labour hours worked producing Meg dolls were 12,000 hours.

- 36,000 Meg dolls were produced with a material cost for pink plastic of £39,200.

TASK 1.5

Use the data from task 1.4 to calculate the budgeted fixed overhead absorption rate for the manufacturing department for November.

TASK 1.6

Use the information from tasks 1.3 and 1.5 to complete the table below to show:

(a)   the total cost of production;

(b)   the unit cost of production of a Meg doll for November.

Product: Meg doll	£
Direct costs	
Pink plastic	
Direct labour	
Indirect costs	
Manufacturing department overheads	
Total cost of production	
Number of Meg dolls produced	
Unit cost of production (to the nearest penny)	

SECTION 2

You should spend about 90 minutes on this section.

DATA

In addition to producing Meg dolls, the company manufactures and sells three types of doll house, products E, C and R. The expected monthly costs and sales information for each product is as follows:

Product	E	C	R
Sales and production units	2,000	1,500	500
Machine hours per month	200	225	175
Total sales revenue	£60,000	£60,000	£30,000
Total direct materials	£20,000	£16,500	£6,000
Total direct labour	£32,000	£24,000	£10,000
Total variable overheads	£4,000	£2,625	£3,500

The total expected monthly fixed costs relating to the production of all doll houses are £4,800.

TASK 2.1

Complete the table below to show for each product the expected contribution per unit.

Product	E £	C £	R £
Selling price per unit			
Less: Unit variable costs			
Direct materials			
Direct labour			
Variable overheads			
Contribution per unit			

TASK 2.2

If the company only manufactures product E, calculate the number of units it would need to make and sell each month to cover the fixed costs of £4,800.

ADDITIONAL DATA

The breakdown of a machine used in the manufacture of doll houses has reduced available machine time from 600 to 365 hours. The Finance Director asks you to calculate the contribution of each doll house per machine hour.

TASK 2.3

Use the data from task 2.1 to complete the table below.

Product	E	C	R
Contribution per unit			
Machine hours per unit			
Contribution per machine hour			

TASK 2.4

Use the data from Task 2.3 to calculate how many units of products E, C and R the company should make and sell to maximize its profits using 365 machine hours.

ADDITIONAL DATA

The company requires an annual rate of return of 10% on any new project. The Managing Director has asked you to appraise the financial affects of introducing a new doll house. You are given the following information relating to this product:

	Year 1	Year 2	Year 3	Year 4	Year 5
	£000	£000	£000	£000	£000
Design costs	80				
Sales revenues		30	50	160	50
Variable costs		15	25	80	25
10% Present value factor	0.909	0.826	0.751	0.683	0.621

TASK 2.5

Calculate for the new doll house project:

(a)   the payback period,

(b)   the net present value.

TASK 2.6

Use the data from Task 2.5 to prepare a report to the Managing Director on the new doll house project. Your report should:

(a)   identify TWO additional items of information relevant to appraising this project,

(b)   recommend whether to accept or reject the project based on its net present value.

FOULKS LYNCH
PUBLICATIONS

ANSWERS TO PRACTICE ACTIVITIES

INTRODUCTION TO COST ACCOUNTING

ACTIVITY 1

(a) A quantitative unit of product or service to which costs are ascertained.

(b)

Business/Service	Cost unit
Airline	Passenger mile
Accountant's Office	Chargeable hour
Restaurant	Meal/Cover
Hospital	Per Patient Day
Limestone Quarry	Tonne
Brewery	Barrel
University	Per Student
Oil Refinery	Barrel

ACTIVITY 2

High–low method will highlight the variable element of the cost.

	High	Low	Range
Mileage	1,000,000	600,000	400,000
Cost	£150,000	£110,000	£40,000

Variable element per mile

$$= \frac{£40,000}{400,000} = £0.10 \text{ per mile}$$

Fixed element at 600,000 miles

Total cost less variable element = fixed cost

£110,000 − (600,000 × £0.10) = £50,000

Likewise at 1,000,000 miles

= £150,000 − (1,000,000 × £0.10) = £50,000

ORDERING AND ISSUING MATERIALS

ACTIVITY 3

Maximum amount of stock to be held	=	24 + 6	= 30 units
Amount to be ordered	=	30 – 5	= 25 units

ACTIVITY 4

Maximum stock level	1,200 metres
Buffer stock	300 metres
Expected usage in review period	900 metres

The review period must therefore be every three weeks (900 metres/300 metres).

ACTIVITY 5

Re-order level = Maximum demand per day × Maximum lead time in days

$$= \frac{4{,}000}{25} \times 6$$

$$= 960 \text{ units}$$

ACTIVITY 6

	£
	£
Cost of storing stock	3.20
Cost of capital 12% × £140	16.80
	20.00

ACTIVITY 7

Re-order level is:

Maximum demand per day × Maximum lead time in days

$$= \frac{3000}{25} \times 5 \text{ days} = 600 \text{ units}$$

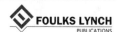

ACTIVITY 8

$$EOQ = \sqrt{\frac{2 \times C_o \times D}{C_h}}$$

$C_o = £45$

$C_h = £1.50$

$D = 150,000$

$$EOQ = \sqrt{\frac{2 \times 45 \times 150,000}{1.5}} = 3,000 \text{ units}$$

ACTIVITY 9

<table>
<tr><td colspan="5" align="center">**PURCHASE ORDER**</td></tr>
<tr><td colspan="2">To: Lynn Paul Ltd</td><td colspan="3">Number: 71443
Date: 5 Oct 200X
Purchase requisition number: P1114</td></tr>
<tr><td colspan="5">Please supply in accordance with attached conditions of purchase.</td></tr>
<tr><td>*Quantity*</td><td>*Description/
code*</td><td>*Delivery
date*</td><td>*Price
£*</td><td>*Per*</td></tr>
<tr><td>100 litres</td><td>JG571</td><td>22 Oct 0X</td><td>16.75</td><td>litre</td></tr>
<tr><td colspan="5">Your quotation: £1,675.00

Authorisation: Purchasing Manager</td></tr>
</table>

ACTIVITY 10

GOODS RECEIVED NOTE

Supplier: Jones Materials Supplies Ltd

Carrier: Smith Deliveries & Co

Date of delivery: 22 Sept 0X

Number: 43719
Date: 22 Sept 0X
Purchase order no: 37523

Description	Code	Quantity	Number of packages
Material	APB2	4,000	40 boxes

Received by: Stores Assistant Manager
Required by: Factory
Accepted by: Stores Assistant Manager
Date: 22 Sept 0X

INSPECTION REPORT

Quantity passed	Quantity rejected	Remarks
40 boxes	-	-

Inspector: Stores Assistant Manager
Date: 22 Sept 0X

ACTIVITY 11

LYNN PAUL LTD – PURCHASE INVOICE	
To: ABC Ltd Date: 22 Oct 200X Purchase order no: 71443	Number: 53533
For supply and delivery of:	£
100 litres JG571 @ £16.75 per litre	1,675.00
Payment due in 14 days	

ACTIVITY 12

STORES LEDGER ACCOUNT

Material…………………………………….. Maximum quantity…………………………………….

Code……………………………………. Minimum quantity…………………………………….

	Receipts					Issues				Stock	
Date	GRN No	Quantity	Unit price £	Amount £	Date	Stores No. Req	Quantity	Amount £	Quantity	Unit price £	Amount £
22 Oct 0X	3325	100 litres	16.75	1,675							

ACTIVITY 13

GOODS RETURNED NOTE			Ref: RET/86
Date returned	Description	Code	Quantity
15 May 0X	4cm Hardwood	HW400	2 metres

Released by: Factory Manager
Accepted by: Storekeeper
Bin card entered: 15 May 200X
Stores ledger card entered: 20 May 200X

FOULKS LYNCH
PUBLICATIONS

BIN CARD

Description……………………………………Location……………………….. Code……………….

Maximum…………….Minimum…………….Reorder level………… Reorder quantity…………

Receipts			Issues			Current stock level	On order		
Date	GRN Ref	Quantity	Date	Issue Ref	Quantity		Date	Ref	Quantity
15/5	RET/ 86	2							

STORES LEDGER ACCOUNT

Material………………………………………..   Maximum quantity…………………………………….

Code………………………………………..   Minimum quantity…………………………………….

Receipts					Issues				Stock		
Date	GRN No	Quantity	Unit price £	Amount £	Date	Stores No. Req	Quantity	Amount £	Quantity	Unit price £	Amount £
15/5	RET/ 86	2									

ACTIVITY 14

Task 1

(i)   **Re-order level** (ROL)   =   Maximum usage × Maximum lead time

=   1,100 × 4

=   4,400 units

(ii)   **Re-order quantity (ROQ)**

Tutorial note:

In the context of this question there are two ways of deriving a re-order quantity.

(1)   Calculate as a balancing figure using the formulae relating to ROL, maximum stock, minimum stock.

(2)   Calculate the cost of using various re-order quantities and select the ROQ which has the lowest associated cost.

In this question it is only possible to use the first approach. We know that ROQ appears in two formulae, the maximum stock level formula and the average stock level formula.

As we have the maximum stock, ROL, minimum usage and minimum lead time we can find the ROQ as the balancing figure in the maximum stock level formula.

Maximum stock level   =   ROL – (Minimum usage × Minimum lead time) + ROQ

5,500   = $4,400 - (900 \times 2) + ROQ$

ROQ   = $5,500 - 4,400 + 1,800 = 2,900$ units

(iii)   Minimum stock level

$$= ROL - (Average\ usage \times Average\ lead\ time)$$

$$= 4,400 - (1,000 \times 3) = 1,400\ units$$

(iv)   Average stock level

either: $$\frac{Maximum\ stock\ level + Minimum\ stock\ level}{2}$$

$$= \frac{5,500 + 1,400}{2} = \underline{3,450\ units}$$

or: Minimum stock level + ½ ROQ

$$= 1,400 + (½ \times 2,900) = \underline{2,850\ units}$$

Tutorial note: both of these formulae are established in recognised textbooks but the latter formula is more widely recognised.

Task 2

Efficient storekeeping should include the following practices (only four were necessary for the question):

(i)   Layout

Gangways wide enough for appropriate handling equipment, location of each item determined logically e.g., by basing on code numbers, to facilitate easy access.

(ii)   Issues

Based on material requisition which has been authorised and on a first-in-first-out basis to ensure old stock used first.

(iii)   Centralised/decentralised

A decision should be made as to the best arrangement to use in each particular case.

(iv)   Goods received

Arrangements should be made to ensure no deliveries are left without a signature from an authorised storekeeper to confirm receipt. Goods must be checked to ensure quality and specification is correct and to ensure claims for breakages are made. Quantities received must be recorded (on a goods received note) so that stock records can be updated and purchase invoices can be cleared for payment.

(v) **Containers/shelves**

These should be designed so as to minimise deterioration or damage to stock while being stored - with appropriate security arrangements for high value items.

(vi) **Continuous stocktaking**

This should be carried out by staff independent from the storekeepers in order to ensure accuracy of the perpetual inventory records to act as a control over the storekeepers.

(vii) **Re-order level and re-order quantity**

These should be established for all stock lines to ensure that re-ordering/replenishment is carried out efficiently. For low value items it may be appropriate to use the 'two bin system'.

(viii) **Slow-moving items**

Periodic checks should be carried out e.g. by calculating stores turnover, to identify and deal with slow-moving or obsolete stocks.

ACTIVITY 15

The documents used in the control and authorisation of materials purchasing procedures include the following:

(1)   Purchase requisition

(2)   Purchase order

(3)   Supplier delivery note

(4)   Goods received note

(5)   Purchase invoice.

ACTIVITY 16

Tutorial note: the question is extremely broad in nature and hence in answering it is necessary to cover all aspects of stock control. Note that a list format is perfectly acceptable.

The essential requirements of an effective material stock control system may be summarised as follows:

(a) **Goods received**

Deliveries should be checked for quantity and quality so incorrect/damaged items are returned. Goods received notes should be prepared to provide a basis for update of stock records and for checking purchase invoices.

(b) **Stores**

Only authorised personnel should be allowed in stores. Stock should be kept in appropriate containers and gangways/shelves designed to allow easy access.

(c)   **Stock records**

Perpetual inventory records should be maintained to provide a continuous record of stock - as a basis for control. These records should be checked for accuracy by, for example, continuous stocktaking (ie, sample of items checked daily and compared with the records).

(d)   **Issues**

Issues from stores should be documented with material requisitions which should be authorised and indicate, if appropriate, which job the material relates to.

(e)   **Stock levels**

Optimum reorder quantities and reorder levels should be calculated for each stock line.

(f)   **Purchasing**

Purchase orders should be authorised and suppliers should be selected by consideration of quality of product, reliability of supply and price.

(g)   **ABC inventory analysis**

This procedure enables different procedures to be adopted for each category of stock. High value items justify use of more sophisticated control procedures.

(h)   **Stores turnover**

Stores turnover ratio = $\dfrac{\text{Quantity issued}}{\text{Average stock}}$

This ratio gives an indication of how much a stock item is used and whether the quantity held is too high.

ACTIVITY 17

(a)   **FIFO Method**

Stores ledger account

	RECEIPTS			ISSUES			BALANCE		
	Units	Price £	£	Units	Price £	£	Units	Price £	£
1 January	50	250	12,500				50	250	12,500
1 February	100	300	30,000				100	300	30,000
							150		42,500
February				50	250	12,500			
				25	300	7,500			
							(75)		(20,000)
							75	300	22,500
1 March	200	292.5	58,500				200	292.5	58,500
1 May	300	285.0	85,500				300	285.0	85,500
							575		166,500
				75	300	22,500			

	Units	Price	£		
May	200	292.5	58,500		
	75	285.0	21,375		
	(350)		(102,375)		
	225	285	64,125		

Closing stock of 225 units is made up of 225 units @ 285 = £64,125

(b) LIFO Method

Stores ledger account

	Receipts			Issues			Balance		
	Units	*Price*	*£*	*Units*	*Price*	*£*	*Units*	*Price*	*£*
1 January	50	250	12,500				50	250	12,500
1 February	100	300	30,000				100	300	30,000
							150		42,500
February				75	300	22,500			
							(75)		(22,500)
							75		20,000
1 March	200	292.5	58,500				200		58,500
1 May	300	285.0	85,500				300		85,500
							575		164,000
				300	285				
May				50	292.5		(350)		100,125
							225		63,875

Closing stock of 225 units is made up of:

	£
150 units @ 292.5	43,875
25 units @ 300	7,500
50 units @ 250	12,500
	63,875

(c) Weighted Average Method

Stores ledger account

	Receipts			Issues			Balance		
	Units	*Price*	*£*	*Units*	*Price*	*£*	*Units*	*£*	*Average Price*
1 January	50	250	12,500				50	12,500	
1 February	100	300	30,000				100	30,000	
							150	42,500	283.33
February				75	283.33	21,250			
							(75)	(21,250)	
							75	21,250	
1 March	200	292.5	58,500				200	58,500	
1 May	300	285.0	85,500				300	85,500	
							575	144,000	250.43

FOULKS LYNCH
PUBLICATIONS

May		350	250.43				
					(350)		(87,650)
					225		56,350

Closing stock of 225 units is made up of: 225 units @ 250.43 = £56,347 (small rounding error)

ACTIVITY 18

LIFO valuation

Date	Receipts			Issues			Balance		
200X	Quantity	Price £	Value £	Quantity	Price £	Value £	Quantity	Price £	Value £
								1,000 at 2.50	
b/f							2,000	500 at 2.00	3,750
								500 at 0.50	
January				1,500	1,000 at 2.50				
					500 at 2.00	3,500	500		250
February	10,000	2.50	25,000				10,500		25,250
March				8,000	8,000 at 2.50	20,000	2,500		5,250
April	15,000	2.60	39,000				17,500		44,250
May	6,500	2.70	17,550				24,000		61,800
June				22,000	6,500 at 2.70		2,000	1,500 at 2.50	
					15,000 at 2.60	57,800		500 at 0.50	4,000
					500 at 2.50				

FIFO valuation

Date	Receipts			Issues			Balance		
200X	Quantity	Price £	Value £	Quantity	Price £	Value £	Quantity	Price £	Value £
b/f							2,000	2.50	5,000
January				1,500	1,500 at 2.50	3,750	500		1,250
February	10,000	2.50	25,000				10,500		26,250
March				8,000	500 at 2.50 7,500 at 2.50	20,000	2,500		6,250
April	15,000	2.60	39,000				17,500		45,250
May	6,500	2.70	17,550				24,000		62,800
June				22,000	2,500 at 2.50 15,000 at 2.60 4,500 at 2.70	57,400	2,000	2.70	5,400

DIRECT LABOUR

ACTIVITY 19

(a) $89 \times £3.50 = £311.50$

(b) $(60 \times £3.00) + (20 \times £3.20) + (9 \times £3.50) = £275.50$

ACTIVITY 20

$£4.40 \times 1.50 = £6.60$

ACTIVITY 21

Annual salary	£16,400
Standard hours to be worked in the year	
(52 weeks × 37.5 hours)	1,950 hours
Salary rate per hour	$\dfrac{£16,400}{1,950}$
	= £8.41 per hour
Overtime rate (2 × £8.41)	= £16.82 per hour
Overtime to be paid in month	
(5 hours × £16.82)	= £84.10

ACTIVITY 22

Bonus (£22,000 × 0.02) = £440

ACTIVITY 23

		£
Basic rate	$\dfrac{18}{60} \times £4.80$	1.44
Bonus	$\dfrac{20-18}{2} \times \dfrac{£4.80}{60}$	0.08
Total payment for job B		1.52

ACTIVITY 24

		£
Basic rate	72 hours × £5.40	388.80
Bonus	$(108 - 72) \times \dfrac{36}{108} \times £5.40$	64.80
Total payment for job		453.60

ACTIVITY 25

TIME SHEET						
Name: Nessa Trandheim				**Clock Number:** NT641		
Department: Factory						
Week commencing: 4 June						

To be completed by employee				For office use		
Day	*Start*	*Finish*	*Job*	*Code*	*Hours*	*£*
Monday	9.00	12.00	Product J			
	1.00	7.00	Product L			
Tuesday	8.00	12.00	Product L			
	1.00	6.00	Product K			
Wednesday	9.00	12.00	Product K			
	1.00	5.00	Product K			
Thursday	8.00	1.00	Product K			
	2.00	5.00	Product K			
Friday	8.00	11.00	Product L			
	12.30	5.30	Product J			
Basic pay						
Overtime premium						____
Gross wages						____

Foreman's signature:

Date:

ACTIVITY 26

COST CARD BATCH 239457	
	£
Materials cost	X
Labour cost	
(25 hours × £6.50)	162.50
(27 units × £2.50)	67.50

COST CARD BATCH 239458	
	£
Materials cost	X
Labour cost	
(23 hours × £6.50)	149.50
(24 units × £2.50)	60.00

ACTIVITY 27

Name	Clock No	Hrs	**Pay**				**Deductions**			
			Basic pay	Overtime premium	Bonus	Gross pay	Tax	NI	Other	Net pay
R Jabasi	289464	39	429.00	22.00	120.12	571.12				

Workings

(W1) Annual salary £20,020

Basic hourly rate	$\dfrac{£20,020}{52\,weeks \times 35\,hours}$	=	£11 per hour
Basic pay	(39 hours × £11)	=	£429.00
Overtime payment		=	£11 × 1.5
		=	£16.50 per hour
Overtime premium	(4 hours × (£16.50 – £11))	=	£22.00

(W2) Bonus   (0.006 × £20,020)   =   £120.12

ACTIVITY 28

The file should contain the following:

(a)   full name, address and next of kin

(b)   previous employment

(c)   clock number issued (if on flexi time basis/hourly paid basis)

(d)   date engaged

(e)   department, job title and pay rate upon engagement

(f)   amendments to (e) above, recorded as and when they occur

(g)   on the termination of employment, the date and reason for leaving.

ACTIVITY 29

(a)   Piecework

80 units	£35.20 (guaranteed minimum wage)
120 units	£36.00
210 units	£63.00

Working

Guaranteed wage	=	80% (8 × 5.50)
	=	£35.20
80 units Standard time 80 × 3	=	240 minutes
∴ Piecework	=	£24
∴ Pay guaranteed wage		
120 units Standard time 120 × 3	=	360 minutes
∴ Piecework	=	£36
210 units Standard time 210 × 3	=	630 minutes
∴ Piecework	=	£63

(b)   Premium bonus

80 units	£44.00
120 units	£44.00
210 units	£54.31

Working

Basic pay   =   8 × £5.50   =   £44

Units	Time taken (minutes)	Time allowed	Saved
80	480	240	
120	480	360	
210	480	630	150

Bonus for 210 units

$$\frac{150}{60} \times 75\% \times £5.50 = £10.31$$

Total wage = £44.00 + £10.31 = £54.31

ACTIVITY 30

Calculation of gross wages

	Operator					
	X		Y		Z	
Standard minutes for actual output:						
Product A	15 × 42 =	630	15 × 42 =	630	15 × 42 =	630
Product B	13 × 60 =	780	10 × 60 =	600	18 × 60 =	1,080
Product C	11 × 75 =	825	8 × 75 =	600	16 × 75 =	1,200
		2,235		1,830		2,910

Attendance time in minutes	$38 \times 60 =$	2,280	$39 \times 60 =$	2,340	$42 \times 60 =$	2,520
$\dfrac{\text{Total standard minutes}}{\text{Attendance time}} \times 100$	$\dfrac{2,235}{2,280} \times 100 =$	98%	$\dfrac{1,830}{2,340} \times 100 =$	78%	$\dfrac{2,910}{2,520} \times 100 =$	115%
Rate per hour		38×4.80		39×4.40		42×5.40
Gross pay		= £182.40		= £171.60		= £226.80

ACTIVITY 31

Halsey 50% of time saved given as a bonus

Job A

		£
Basic payment	$\dfrac{36}{60} \times £4.80$	2.88
Bonus (Time saved $60 - 36 = 24$)	$\dfrac{24}{60} \times \frac{1}{2} \times £4.80$	0.96
		3.84

Rowan Bonus is based on time taken as a percentage of time allowed

Job A

		£
Basic payment	$\dfrac{36}{60} \times £4.80$	2.88
Bonus (Time saved 24 minutes)	$\dfrac{36}{60} \times \dfrac{24}{60} \times £4.80$	1.15
		4.03

ACTIVITY 32

Time based schemes, as the name suggests, involve the calculation of remuneration on the basis of time spent by employees and not linking that remuneration to productive work done or output produced. This will normally be at an agreed basic rate for a standard working week - in this case 40 hours. Hours in excess of this will then be paid as overtime at a higher rate. The existing scheme operated by A Ltd is an example - wages being paid at £4 per hour. It is also possible to incorporate premiums for shift working.

The advantages of time-based schemes are:

(a)   they are appropriate for indirect workers

(b)   they should be used for direct operatives who cannot influence the rate of output - this is the case when workers are operating an automated or semi-automated production line or where team-working is necessary (an important feature of A Ltd is that the employees work independently which makes it feasible to introduce a performance-related scheme)

(c)   they are most appropriate where quality of output is a key priority

(d)   the schemes are easier to understand and to administer.

Performance-based remuneration systems involve linking wages earned to the level of output produced. This may be done by basic pay being paid on a time basis and bonuses paid if output exceeds pre-determined targets. Alternatively a piece rate system can be used. In the case of A Ltd this is a differential piece rate system with a guaranteed minimum which is designed to protect employees' earnings from factors outside their control (e.g. stock-outs).

The main merits of performance-based systems are:

(a) less supervision should be necessary

(b) employees have an incentive to earn more in order to increase output: this increased output — assuming that it can be sold — will result in increased profit

(c) by spending less time per unit, savings should be achieved in labour-related variable overheads.

A cost comparison can be made as follows:

Existing scheme

Output per employee	=	$\dfrac{6,000}{6}$
	=	1,000
Current basic wage per week	=	£4 × 40
	=	£160
∴ Average cost per unit	=	$\dfrac{£160}{1,000}$
	=	16 pence

Proposed scheme

Output per employee	=	$\dfrac{6,600}{6}$
	=	1,100 units

Expected wage per employee

	=	800 × 0.16	=	128
	+	200 × 0.17	=	34
	+	100 × 0.18	=	18
	=			£180

Average cost per unit	=	$\dfrac{£180}{1,100}$
	=	16.4 pence

The proposed scheme offers employees the opportunity to earn at least the same amount per unit ie, 16p but with potential to increase their weekly wage from £160 to £180. This assumes that the output level of 6,600 units is a reasonable estimate of what the employees can achieve. A potential problem with the scheme is that the guaranteed wage is effectively reduced from £160 to £140 which may not be acceptable.

DIRECT AND INDIRECT EXPENSES

ACTIVITY 33

(a) Contract or job

(b) Therm

(c) Tonne/ton or sheet

(d) Enrolled student or successful student

(e) Calls made or orders taken

(f) Call answered or transfer made

Conclusion A cost unit is simply the unit chosen by an organisation for which it will gather together all of the relevant costs. It might be one individual unit of output or a batch of units of output.

ACTIVITY 34

Variable costs per circuit board

	£
Materials	60
Labour	20
	80

The variable cost is £80 per circuit board.

Fixed costs per annum

Factory rent	20,000
Business rates	4,000
Production director's salary	24,000
	48,000

The fixed costs for the business are £48,000 each year.

Conclusion The materials and labour used in a product will tend to be variable costs as they will increase if production levels rise and decrease if production levels fall. The expenses of the business will tend to be split between fixed and variable expenses. Some such as factory rentals will be clearly fixed whereas others such as machine power will vary with levels of production.

ACTIVITY 35

The total life of the machine in hours is estimated to be 9,000 hours (5,400 + 3,600). The hours used this year were 1,200.

$$\text{Depreciation charge} \quad = \quad \frac{1,200}{9,000} \times £47,000 = \quad £6,267$$

ACTIVITY 36

Tutorial note:

(1)   A fairly straightforward question on fundamental cost accounting topics.

(2)   Most of task 1 is obvious and students should be able to gain a majority of the marks using very little time.

(3)   Task 2 requires some thought.

Task 1

Ref No	Production overhead	Selling & dist overhead	Admin overhead	R&D overhead
1	x			
2		x		
3	x			
4				x
5		x		
6			x	
7		x		
8	x			
9	x			
10		x		
11		x		
12				x
13			x	
14	x			
15			x	
16	x			

Task 2

Direct production labour costs are treated as fixed because:

(i)   workers are often paid on a time basis and have secured, guaranteed wages

(ii)   employees are not hired and fired with small changes in activity – in this way they tend to be more a type of 'stepped cost', not a true variable cost

(iii) bonuses and other incentives invalidate uniform unit cost assumptions.

ACTIVITY 37

(a)   **All direct costs are variable**

This is not necessarily true. A direct cost is a cost which can be directly attributable to a unit of production or a cost centre. Where costs are attributed to a unit of production they will be variable, although discounts for volume will perhaps affect the linearity of this relationship. Where costs are attributable to cost centres, there will be direct costs which are not variable. For instance, where process costing is used, the process manager's wages will be a direct cost of the process, but will be a fixed cost. A similar case can be made for depreciation of process plant.

(b) **Variable costs are controllable and fixed costs are not**

This is not always so. While it is probably true that most variable costs are controllable and many fixed are not, there is no direct relationship between the two classifications. Costs may be classified into fixed and variable, depending on their behaviour when output levels fluctuate. Costs may also be classified into controllable and uncontrollable, depending on the circumstances, the authority of the individual and the time span being considered e.g., depreciation can be treated as a fixed cost or a variable cost. It is usually charged on a time basis and treated as fixed, but it can be charged on a usage basis and treated as variable. Depreciation will be uncontrollable to the process supervisor, but may be regarded as controllable in the long-term by the process manager who authorises capital expenditure, but once purchased, is uncontrollable by him in the short-term.

APPORTIONMENT OF INDIRECT COSTS

ACTIVITY 38

	Department X £
Insurance (based on floor area)	
$\dfrac{1{,}200}{1{,}200 + 400} \times £1{,}600$	1,200
Depreciation (based on value of machinery)	
$\dfrac{£64{,}000}{£64{,}000 + £32{,}000} \times £17{,}400$	11,600
Maintenance department costs (based on number of callouts)	
$\dfrac{12}{12 + 24} \times £21{,}000$	7,000

	Department Y £
Insurance (based on floor area)	
$\dfrac{400}{1{,}200 + 400} \times £1{,}600$	400
Depreciation (based on value of machinery)	
$\dfrac{£32{,}000}{£64{,}000 + £32{,}000} \times £17{,}400$	5,800
Maintenance department costs (based on number of callouts)	
$\dfrac{24}{12 + 24} \times £21{,}000$	14,000

ACTIVITY 39

Task 1

OVERHEAD ANALYSIS SHEET				DATE:		
	TOTAL	PRODUCTION			SERVICE	
		Assembly	Machining	Finishing	Maint.	Canteen
	£	£	£	£	£	£
Total overhead	60,000	19,050	16,275	11,437	5,175	8,063
Apportion maintenance Basis: value of machinery						
200/430 × £5,175		2,407			(5,175)	
180/430 × £5,175			2,166			
50/430 × £5,175				602		
Apportion canteen costs Basis: number of employees						
50/100 × £8,063		4,031				(8,063)
30/100 × £8,063			2,419			
20/100 × £8,063				1,613		
Total overhead	60,000	25,488	20,860	13,652		

Tutorial note: If the assumption is made that the service cost centres do not service each other then it does not matter which service cost centre costs are apportioned first. Therefore in this activity the same result would have been reached if the canteen had been apportioned before the maintenance department.

Task 2

OVERHEAD ANALYSIS SHEET					DATE:	
	TOTAL	PRODUCTION			SERVICE	
	£	Assembly £	Machining £	Finishing £	Maint. £	Canteen £
Total overhead	60,000	19,050	16,275	11,437	5,175	8,063
Apportion canteen costs Basis: number of employees						
50/105 × £8,063		3,839				(8,063)
30/105 × £8,063			2,304			
20/105 × £8,063				1,536		
5/105 × £8,063					384	
		22,889	18,579	12,973	5,559 (5,559)	NIL
Apportion maintenance Basis: value of machinery						
200/460 × £5,559		2,417				
180/460 × £5,559			2,175			
50/460 × £5,559				604		
30/460 × £5,559						363
		25,306	20,754	13,577	NIL	363
Reapportion canteen costs		173	104	69	17	(363)
Allocate maintenance costs		25,479	20,858	13,646	17	NIL
		7	6	4	(17)	–
		25,486	20,864	13,650	NIL	NIL

OVERHEAD ABSORPTION

ACTIVITY 40

(i)

	Hours	
	Cutting	*Assembly*
Number of labour hours expected to be worked		
XJ1 2.5 hours × 20,000 units	50,000	
XJ1 0.75 hours × 20,000 units		15,000
XJ2 1 hour × 10,000 units	10,000	
XJ2 1 hour × 10,000 units		10,000
	60,000	25,000
Total overhead	£67,000	£42,000

Overhead absorption rate

$$\frac{£67,000}{60,000 \text{ hours}}$$ £1.12 per labour hour

$$\frac{£42,000}{25,000 \text{ hours}}$$ £1.68 per labour hour

(ii)   Overheads included in the cost of each product

Product XJ1			£
Cutting	2.5 hours ×	£1.12	2.80
Assembly	0.75 hours ×	£1.68	1.26
			4.06

Product XJ2			
Cutting	1 hour ×	£1.12	1.12
Assembly	1 hour ×	£1.68	1.68
			2.80

Conclusion   Absorption of overheads on the basis of labour hours is most appropriate in production departments that are largely labour based departments.

ACTIVITY 41

(i)   Total material input cost

	Production department	
	I	*II*
	£	£
Product X		
£1.20 × 10,000 units	12,000	
£9.30 × 10,000 units		93,000
Product Y		
£24.50 × 6,000 units	147,000	
£10.80 × 6,000 units		64,800
	———	———
	£159,000	£157,800
	———	———
Total overhead	£46,000	£75,000

Overhead absorption rate

$$\frac{£46,000}{£159,000}$$ £0.29 per £ of direct material input

$$\frac{£75,000}{£157,800}$$ £0.48 per £ of direct material input

(ii) Overhead absorbed by each product

	£
Product X	
Dept I: 1.2 × £0.29	0.348
Dept II: 9.3 × £0.48	4.464
	———
	4.812
	———
Product Y	
Dept I: 24.5 × £0.29	7.105
Dept II: 10.8 × £0.48	5.184
	———
	12.289
	———

ACTIVITY 42

Total machine hours for machine shop

Product J	
4 hours × 20,000 units	80,000
Product K	
6 hours × 30,000 units	180,000
	———
	260,000
Machine shop overhead	£269,000

Overhead absorption rate

$$\frac{£269,000}{260,000 \text{ hours}} \quad = \quad £1.04 \text{ per machine hour}$$

Total labour hours for polishing department

Product J 4 hours × 20,000 units	80,000
Product K 3 hours × 30,000 units	90,000
	170,000

Polishing department overhead   £240,000

Overhead absorption rate

$$\frac{£240,000}{170,000 \text{ hours}} \quad = \quad £1.41 \text{ per labour hour}$$

Total labour cost for finishing department

	£'000	£'000
Product J		
Grade B 8 hours × £8.70 × 20,000 units	1,392	
Grade C 1 hour × £6.40 × 20,000 units	128	
		1,520
Product K		
Grade C 6 hours × £6.40 × 30,000 units	1,152	
Grade A 2 hours × £10.10 × 30,000 units	606	
		1,758
		3,278

Overhead absorption rate

$$\frac{£170,000}{£3,278,000} \quad = \quad £0.05 \text{ per £ of direct labour cost}$$

Overheads included in the cost of each product

	£
Product J	
Machine shop 4 hours × £1.04	4.16
Polishing 4 hours × £1.41	5.64
Finishing $\dfrac{£1,520,000}{20,000}$	
= 76 × £0.05	3.80
	13.60

Product K
Machine shop 6 hours × £1.04   6.24
Polishing 3 hours × £1.41   4.23

Finishing $\dfrac{£1,758,000}{30,000}$

= 58.6 × £0.05   2.93
                                                                                           ‾‾‾‾
                                                                                           13.40
                                                                                           ‾‾‾‾

ACTIVITY 43

Standard overhead absorption rate   = $\dfrac{£14,000}{28,000 \text{ hours}}$

                                           =   £0.50 per hour

                                                                                      £
Overhead absorbed into units of production
 25,000 hours × £0.50   12,500
Overhead incurred   12,000
                                                                                   ‾‾‾‾‾‾
Over absorption of overhead   500
                                                                                   ‾‾‾‾‾‾

Causes of over absorption:
Expenditure
 (£12,000 – £14,000)   2,000
Volume
 (28,000 – 25,000 hours) × £0.50   (1,500)
                                                                                   ‾‾‾‾‾‾
                                                                                      500
                                                                                   ‾‾‾‾‾‾

Since actual overhead is £2,000 less budgeted overhead, this could lead to an over absorption of overhead. This factor is offset partially by actual hours being less than budgeted hours and therefore less overhead being absorbed.

ACTIVITY 44

Product cost - book

                                                                                      £
Print   1.50
Print overhead $\dfrac{15}{60} \times \dfrac{£8,000}{20,000}$ 0.10

Binding   0.75
Binding overhead $\dfrac{30}{60} \times \dfrac{£12,000}{30,000}$ 0.20

Jacket & finishing   0.30
Finishing overhead $\dfrac{15}{60} \times \dfrac{£6,000}{5,000}$ 0.30
                                                                                    ‾‾‾‾
Total cost   3.15
                                                                                    ‾‾‾‾

ACTIVITY 45

(i)   **Tutorial note:**

The stages to follow in calculating the absorption rate are:

(1)   Find budgeted overhead for each cost centre. Note: it is vital to state the basis of apportionment.

(2)   Reapportion the service cost centres. As the canteen provides benefit to the maintenance department not vice versa it is quicker to reapportion the canteen first.

(3)   Calculate the budgeted units of base (eg, machine hours, labour hours, etc) for each production cost centre.

(4)   The overhead absorption rates can now be calculated.

Budgeted overhead for each cost centre

Overhead	Basis of apportionment	Machine shop	Fitting section	Canteen	Machine maintenance section	Total
		£	£	£	£	
Allocated overheads	(given)	27,660	19,470	16,600	26,650	90,380
Rent, rates, heat and light	Floor area	9,000	3,500	2,500	2,000	17,000
Depreciation and insurance of equipment	Gross book value of equipment	12,500	6,250	2,500	3,750	25,000
		49,160	29,220	21,600	32,400	
Canteen	Number of employees	10,800	8,400	(21,600)	2,400	
Machine maintenance	70 : 30	24,360	10,440		(34,800)	
		84,320	48,060			132,380

Total machine hours in machine shop:

X	6 × 4,200	25,200
Y	3 × 6,900	20,700
Z	4 × 1,700	6,800
		52,700

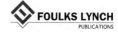

Direct wage cost of fitting section:

		£
X	4,200 × 12	50,400
Y	6,900 × 3	20,700
Z	1,700 × 21	35,700
		£106,800

	Machine shop	Fitting section
Overhead absorption rates	$\dfrac{84,320}{52,700}$	$\dfrac{48,060}{106,800} \times 100$
$\dfrac{\text{Budgeted overhead}}{\text{Budgeted units of base}}$	£1.60 per machine hour	45% of direct wages

(ii) **Calculation of budgeted manufacturing overhead cost per unit of Product X**

		£
Machine shop	6 × 1.60	9.60
Fitting section	12 × 45%	5.40
		15.00

ACTIVITY 46

Task 1

Calculation of overhead absorption rates

	Department	Machine area		Finishing shop	
(i)	**Labour hours**				
	P	$\dfrac{10}{5} \times 6,000$	12,000	$\dfrac{6}{4} \times 6,000$	9,000
	Q	$\dfrac{5}{5} \times 8,000$	8,000	$\dfrac{4}{4} \times 8,000$	8,000
	R	$\dfrac{10}{5} \times 2,000$	4,000	$\dfrac{8}{4} \times 2,000$	4,000
			24,000		21,000

Overhead absorption rate:

$\dfrac{\text{Budgeted overhead}}{\text{Budgeted hours}}$	$\dfrac{100,800}{24,000}$	$\dfrac{94,500}{21,000}$
	= £4.20 per labour hour	= £4.50 per labour hour

(ii) **Machine hours**

P	4 × 6,000	24,000	0.5 × 6,000	3,000
Q	1.5 × 8,000	12,000	0.5 × 8,000	4,000
R	3 × 2,000	6,000	1 × 2,000	2,000
		42,000		9,000

Overhead absorption	$\dfrac{100,800}{42,000}$		$\dfrac{94,500}{9,000}$
	= £2.40 per machine hour		= £10.50 per machine hour

Task 2

Calculation of total cost of each product

		P		Q		R	
			£		£		£
(i)	**Labour hour rate**						
	Materials and wages per question		34.50		24.00		40.50
	Fixed overhead:						
	Machining	2 × 4.20	8.40	1 × 4.20	4.20	2 × 4.20	8.40
	Finishing shop	1.5 × 4.50	6.75	1 × 4.50	4.50	2 × 4.50	9.00
	Total cost		49.65		32.70		57.90
(ii)	**Machine hours**						
	Materials and wages		34.50		24.00		40.50
	Fixed overhead:						
	Machining	4 × 2.40	9.60	1.5 × 2.40	3.60	3 × 2.40	7.20
	Finishing shop	0.5 × 10.50	5.25	0.5 × 10.50	5.25	1 × 10.50	10.50
	Total cost		49.35		32.85		58.20

Task 3

The aim of calculating overhead absorption rates is to calculate as fairly as possible an average cost per unit figure. This is done by selecting the measure of the activity level which fairly reflects the incidence of the overheads. In this context the more appropriate bases to select would be machine hours for the machining department and labour hours for the finishing shop. It would not be as accurate to use a single blanket rate for both departments though it may be acceptable to do so if the effect on the cost per unit figures is not significant.

CODING AND ACCOUNTING FOR COSTS

ACTIVITY 47

Task 1

(a) 1120202

(b) 1224204

(c) 1821209

Task 2

A coding system has the following advantages:

(i)   provides a quick means of referring to individual cost items

(ii)   reduces time involved in writing descriptions

(iii)   should avoid ambiguity;

(iv)   should aid data processing, especially input of data.

Note: Only two advantages were required by the activity.

ACTIVITY 48

Code 384 represents stationery used in the accounts department.

Code 293 represents petrol used by the sales department.

Code 172 represents packaging material used in the packaging department.

ACTIVITY 49

Bank account

		£			£
1 July	Balance b/d	18,500			
31 Oct	Sales	28,750	31 Oct	Stores ledger control	12,000
				Wages clearing	10,830
				Factory overhead	4,200
				Administrative and	
				selling cost	4,250
				Balance c/d	15,970
		47,250		(balance fig)	47,250

Stores ledger control account

		£			£
1 July	Balance b/d	2,125	31 Oct	Work-in-progress	12,500
31 Oct	Bank	12,000		Factory overhead	1,000
				Balance c/d (bal fig)	625
		14,125			14,125

Wages clearing account

		£			£
31 Oct	Bank	10,830	31 Oct	Factory overhead	600
				Work-in-progress (bal fig)	10,230
		10,830			10,830

Finished goods stock control account

		£			£
1 July	Balance b/d	1,500	31 Oct	Factory cost of sales	22,500
31 Oct	Work-in-progress control	24,000		Balance c/d (bal fig)	3,000
		25,500			25,500

Work-in-progress control account

		£			£
1 July	Balance b/d	2,000	31 Oct	Finished goods stock control	24,000
31 Oct	Stores ledger control	12,500			
	Factory overhead	5,800		Balance c/d (bal fig)	6,530
	Wages clearing	10,230			
		30,530			30,530

Factory overhead control account

'Incurred'		£	'Absorbed'		£
31 Oct	Stores ledger	1,000	31 Oct	Work-in-progress control	5,800
	Wages clearing	600			
	Bank	4,200		(No under/over absorption)	
		5,800			5,800

Costing, profit and loss account for the four months ending 31 October

	£		£
Factory cost of sales	22,500	Sales	28,750
Administrative and selling cost	4,250		
Profit	2,000		
	28,750		28,750

ACTIVITY 50

Task 1

(a) (i) **Design principles**

(1) The system should be simple, logical and easily understood.

(2) It should be constructed to prevent duplication and to control the variety of stock items.

(3) The arrangement of code groups and sub-classifications should relate to the needs of the company.

(4) It should be flexible enough to incorporate changes in the pattern of materials stockholding without incurring a fundamental change in the coding system.

(ii) **Advantages**

(1) Each item of material is assigned a unique code, thereby reducing the risk of duplicating the orders for items with similar descriptions.

(2) Logical classification and coding assists the physical functions of storing and identifying materials.

(3) Grouping of related items and coding is inherent to computerisation of stock records and management reporting.

(4) Use of code, instead of a possible lengthy description, saves clerical work in preparing source documents and prevents ambiguity.

(b) It may be interpreted from the examples given that the materials coding structure represents

1st and 2nd digits	raw material, 01 aluminium to 04 stainless steel
3rd and 4th digits	length in 6" gradations
5th and 6th digits	thickness in $\frac{1}{16}$" gradations
7th and 8th digits	width in $\frac{1}{4}$" gradations

Task 2

Code number/fields

Material	Material code	Length (6")	Thickness ($\frac{1}{16}$")	Width ($\frac{1}{4}$")	
Aluminium	01	13	04	14	
Copper		03	02	06	13

Task 3

Code	Material	Length	Thickness	Width
01112903	Aluminium	5'6"	$1\frac{13}{16}$"	$\frac{3}{4}$"
03071721	Copper	3'6"	$1\frac{1}{16}$"	$5\frac{1}{4}$"

JOB AND BATCH COSTING

ACTIVITY 51

Job costing is used when a single item is represented by the cost unit. Costs are thus collected in respect of this single item.

Batch costing is used when a number of identical items are produced for the same customer (or for stock). In these circumstances the batch is the cost unit, and the total cost of the batch is collected. If the cost per individual unit is required, then an average cost is calculated.

PROCESS COSTING

ACTIVITY 52

	Tonnes
Input	4,000
Normal loss	160
Output expected	3,840
Actual output	3,800
Abnormal loss	40

ACTIVITY 53

	Tonnes
Input	5,000
Normal loss	250
Output expected	4,750
Actual output	4,900
Abnormal gain	150

ACTIVITY 54

Euromix

January X3

Process account

	Units	£		Units	£
Raw materials	3,000	6,000	Ouput	2,750	9,220
Direct labour		1,200	Normal loss	150	45
Process overhead		2,400	Abnormal loss	100	335
	3,000	9,600		3,000	9,600

Normal cost of normal production

$$\frac{£9,600 - £45}{2,850}$$

$= £3.35263$

Normal loss account

	Units	£		Units	£
Process %	150	45	Cash or/ debtors	150	45

Abnormal loss account

	Units	£		Units	£
Process a/c	100	335	Cash or debtors	100	30
			Profit and loss a/c		305
		£335			£335

ACTIVITY 55

Euromix 2

February X3

Process account

	Units	£		Units	£
Raw materials	3,500	7,000	Ouput	3,425	10,864
Direct labour		1,200	Normal loss	175	53
Process overhead		2,400			
Abnormal gain	100	317			
	3,600	£10,917		3,600	£10,917

Normal cost of normal production

$$\frac{£10,600 - £53}{3,325}$$

= £3.17203

Normal loss account

	Units	£		Units	£
Process %	175	53	Cash or/ debtors	75	23
			Proft and loss a/c	100	30
	175	£53		175	£53

Abnormal loss account

	Units	£		Units	£
Profit and loss a/c	100	317	Process a/c	100	317
	100	£317		100	£317

MARGINAL COSTING

ACTIVITY 56

Yorkscost Ltd

Operating statement for six months ended 30 June X1

(Absorption basis)

	£
Sales	252,000
Less cost of production	
Direct materials	60,000
Direct labour	45,000
Variable overhead	25,000
Fixed overhead	35,000
Cost of production	165,000
Gross profit	87,000
Variable selling, distribution and admin costs	37,500
Fixed selling, distribution and admin costs	25,000
	62,500
Profit for period	£24,500

Yorkscost Ltd

Operating statement for six months ended 30 June X1

(Marginal costing basis)

	£
Sales	252,000
Less variable costs	
Direct materials	60,000
Direct labour	45,000
Variable production overhead	25,000
Variable selling, distribution and admin costs	37,500
	167,500
Contribution	84,500

Fixed overheads

Production overhead	35,000
Selling distribution and admin costs	25,000
	60,000
Profit for period	£24,500

ACTIVITY 57

Hockeystrike Ltd

Operating statements

Marginal costing principle

	£
Sales	
900 units @ £95	85,500
Less cost of production	
1000 units @ £40	40,000
Closing stocks	
100 units @ £40	(4,000)
	36,000
Contribution	49,500
Fixed costs	25,000
Profit for period	£24,500

Absorption costing principle

	£
Sales	
900 units @ £95	85,500
Cost of production	
(1000 units @ £40 + £25,000)	65,000
Closing stocks	
(100 units @ £65)	(6,500)
Cost of sales	58,500
Net profit for period	£27,000

CVP ANALYSIS, BREAK-EVEN ANALYSIS AND THE LIMITING FACTOR

ACTIVITY 58

Break-even point in units (tonnage) per month

$$\frac{\text{Fixed costs}}{\text{Contribution per unit}}$$

$$= \frac{£60,000}{£30}$$

= 2,000 tonnes per month

Margin of safety

Capacity 6,000 tonnes

Break-even point 2,000 tonnes

Margin of safety 4,000 tonnes

$$\frac{4,000}{6,000} \times \frac{100}{1} = \underline{67\%}$$

ACTIVITY 59

Break-even point in sales value

$$= \frac{\text{Fixed costs}}{(\text{Contribution}/\text{Sales})}$$

$$= \frac{£360,000}{(1,180/3,780)}$$

$$= \underline{£1,153,220} = 31\% \text{ capacity}$$

FOULKS LYNCH
PUBLICATIONS

Profit volume graph

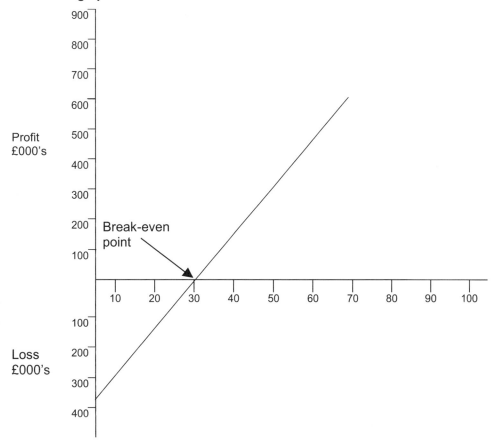

ACTIVITY 60

Contribution per unit of output

	£
Selling price per tonne	105
Variable cost per tonne	75
Contribution per tonne	£30

Revised fixed costs:

£375,000

Target profit £1m

∴ Target contribution

= profit + fixed costs

= £1,000,000 + £380,000

= £1,380,000

Revised volume = $\dfrac{£1,380,000}{£30}$

= £46,000

INVESTMENT APPRAISAL

ACTIVITY 61

Ravenscar Chemical Ltd

Payback period machine in blending process

		Cash flow £	Cumulative cash flow £
YR	1	40,000	40,000
	2	60,000	100,000
	3	30,000	130,000
	4	30,000	160,000
	5	25,000	185,000

Payback period:

$$2 \text{ years} + \left(\frac{25}{30} \times 12 \right)$$

2 years 10 months

DCF schedule

YR	(Outflow) £	Inflow £	NPV Factor	NPV
0	(125,000)		1.00	(125,000)
1		40,000	0.870	34,800
2		60,000	0.757	45,420
3		30,000	0.658	19,740
4		30,000	0.573	17,190
5		25,000	0.498	12,450
			Net present value	£4,600

ACTIVITY 62

Ravenscar Chemical Ltd

The machine for the blending process will payback within less than three years. The project has been discounted at 15% - the company's cost of capital and has a positive net present value which indicates that it is achieving a rate of return of at least 15% and therefore the management should invest in the machine as it has met the desired criteria.

ANSWERS TO SPECIMEN SIMULATION

TASK 1

<table>
<tr><td colspan="13" align="center">STORES RECORD CARD</td></tr>
<tr>
<td colspan="5">Materials description:
Code no:</td>
<td colspan="4">Candlewick thread, 200 metre rolls
CW728</td>
<td colspan="4">Maximum quantity: 400
Minimum quantity: 140
Reorder level: 230
Reorder quantity: 80</td>
</tr>
<tr>
<td></td>
<td colspan="4" align="center">Receipts</td>
<td colspan="4" align="center">Issues</td>
<td colspan="3" align="center">Stock balance</td>
</tr>
<tr>
<td>Date 2003</td>
<td>Document number</td>
<td>Qty</td>
<td>Price per roll (£)</td>
<td>Total (£)</td>
<td>Document number</td>
<td>Qty</td>
<td>Price per roll (£)</td>
<td>Total (£)</td>
<td>Qty</td>
<td>Price per roll (£)</td>
<td>Total (£)</td>
</tr>
<tr>
<td>1 Oct</td><td></td><td></td><td></td><td></td><td></td><td></td><td></td><td></td>
<td>28
26
54</td><td>2.20
2.30</td><td>61.60
59.80
121.40</td>
</tr>
<tr>
<td>3 Oct</td><td></td><td></td><td></td><td></td>
<td>249</td><td>26
4
30</td><td>2.30
2.20</td><td>59.80
8.80
68.60</td>
<td>24</td><td>2.20</td><td>52.80</td>
</tr>
<tr>
<td>6 Oct</td><td>419</td><td>80</td><td>2.35</td><td>188.00</td><td></td><td></td><td></td><td></td>
<td>24
80
104</td><td>2.20
2.35</td><td>52.80
188.00
240.80</td>
</tr>
<tr>
<td>8 Oct</td><td></td><td></td><td></td><td></td>
<td>252</td><td>40</td><td>2.35</td><td>94.00</td>
<td>24
40
64</td><td>2.20
2.35</td><td>5.280
94.00
146.80</td>
</tr>
<tr>
<td>9 Oct</td><td>427</td><td>80</td><td>2.38</td><td>190.40</td><td></td><td></td><td></td><td></td>
<td>24
40
80
144</td><td>2.20
2.35
2.38</td><td>52.80
94.00
190.40
337.20</td>
</tr>
<tr>
<td>10 Oct</td><td>75</td><td>3</td><td>2.35</td><td>7.05</td><td></td><td></td><td></td><td></td>
<td>24
43
80
147</td><td>2.20
2.35
2.38</td><td>52.80
101.05
190.40
344.25</td>
</tr>
</table>

TASK 2

MATERIALS REQUISITION			
Department: Manufacturing		Document no: 252 Date: 08/10/20X3	
Code no	Description	Quantity	**Cost office use only** Value of issue (£)
CW728	Candlewick thread, 200m rolls	40	94.00
Signature:		Received by:	

MATERIALS RETURNED			
Department: Manufacturing		Document no: 275 Date: 10/10/20X3	
Code no	Description	Quantity	**Cost office use only** Value of issue (£)
CW728	Candlewick thread, 200m rolls	3	7.05
Signature:		Received by:	

TASK 3

MEMO

To:	General Manager
From:	Bobby Forster, Accounts Assistant
Date:	14 October 20X3
Subject:	**Stock levels of candlewick thread, week ending 10 October 20X3**

The stock levels on this item have been a cause for concern during the last week.

The stock level began the week below the minimum quantity of 140 rolls and, although two deliveries brought the balance to 147 rolls by the end of the week, it is clear that the minimum level is soon to be reached once more.

This could lead to the company running out of stock before a new batch of candlewick is received from the supplier. Customer orders could be lost or it may be necessary to pay high prices to acquire urgent supplies.

I suggest that we should review the stock control levels and reorder quantity. Perhaps usage patterns have changed since the levels were set. If this is the case the levels and the reorder quantity should be recalculated, taking account of any changes in usage patterns and supply lead times.

I would be happy to discuss the problem with you at any time.

TASK 4

QUALITY CANDLES LIMITED
PIECEWORK OPERATION CARD

Operative name: Mary Roberts   Department: Manufacturing

Clock number: R27

Week beginning: 6 October 20X3

	Mon	**Tues**	**Wed**	**Thurs**	**Fri**
Batches produced	120	102	34	202	115
Batches rejected	5	7	4	11	5
Batches accepted	115	95	30	191	110
Rate per batch	£ 0.50	£ 0.50	£ 0.50	£ 0.50	£ 0.50
Piecework payment	£ 57.50	£47.50	£15.00	£95.50	£55.00
Bonus payable	£2.30	£ nil	£ nil	£ nil	£2.20
Total payable for day*	£59.30	£50.00	£50.00	£95.50	£57.20

Total wages payable for week:

          £

Direct wages   308.00

Indirect wages   4.50

Total wages   <u>312.50</u>

*   Guaranteed daily wage of £50 is payable if piecework payment plus bonus amounts to less than £50.

Supervisor's signature: A Peters

FOULKS LYNCH
PUBLICATIONS

TASK 5

INTERNAL MEMO

To: Roy Hart, Manufacturing Department Supervisor

From: Bobby Forster, Accounts Assistant

Date: 10 October 20X3

Subject: Discrepancy on piecework operation card

I have a query on a piecework operation card for the week beginning 6 October, a copy of which is attached. The employee concerned is Mary Roberts, clock number R27.

The output recorded for Wednesday is exceptionally low and correspondingly the output for Thursday is very high. It is possible that some of the output for Wednesday was recorded in error for Thursday. This distorts the wages payable because of the guaranteed daily rate.

Could you please look into this for me, to see whether there was in fact a genuine reason for the unusual pattern in output levels.

Thank you for your help.

TASK 6

Production overhead analysis sheet for 20X4

Production overhead item	Total £000	Manufacturing £000	Painting/ finishing £000	Packing £000	Stores £000	Maintenance £000
Indirect labour	98	22	14	11	35	16
	40	12	2	2	12	12
	105	45	15	24	12	9
	31	31				
	40	20	4	12	2	2
	24	11	4	6	2	1
	35	15	5	8	4	3
	48	22	8	12	4	2
	15	5	5	5		
Total department overheads	436	183	57	80	71	45
Apportion maintenance total	-	21	12	9	3	(45)
Apportion stores total	-	36	20	18	(74)	
Total production dept overheads	436	240	89	107		

TASK 7

Working paper

Calculation of production overhead absorption rates for 20X4

Manufacturing department

Machine hour rate   = $\dfrac{£240,000}{200,000}$

                     =   £1.20 per machine hour

Painting and finishing department

Labour hour rate   = $\dfrac{£89,000}{28,000}$

                    =   £3.18 per labour hour

Packing department

Machine hour rate   = $\dfrac{£107,000}{90,000}$

                     =   £1.19 per machine hour

TASK 8

Sample calculations: working paper

Reversing order of service department re-apportionments

Production overhead item	Total £000	Manufacturing £000	Painting/ finishing £000	Packing £000	Stores £000	Maintenance £000
Total department overheads (from task 6)	436	183	57	80	71	45
Apportion stores total	-	27	15	13	(71)	16
Apportion maintenance total	-	31	17	13	-	(61)
Total production dept overheads	436	241	89	106		

TASK 9

INTERNAL MEMO

To: General Manager

From: Bobby Forster, Accounts Assistant

Date: 5 November 20X3

Subject: Re-apportionment of service department costs

I have carried out the analysis you requested and the results are attached.

As you will see, the change in method does not result in a material difference in the total overhead for each production cost centre. Therefore I suggest that we should not change our apportionment methods since the value of the management information would not be materially affected by the change.

TASK 10

Journal entry for production overheads

October 20X3

Entries for overhead absorbed during the month

	Debit (£)	Credit (£)
Work in progress: manufacturing dept	18,500	
Work in progress: painting and finishing	7,400	
Work in progress: packing dept	8,300	
Production overhead control		34,200

Entries for overhead under/over absorbed during the month

	Debit (£)	Credit (£)
Overhead over/under absorbed (P+L)	18,400	
Production overhead control		18,400

TASK 10, CONTINUED

INTERNAL MEMO

To: Production Manager

From: Bobby Forster, Accounts Assistant

Date: 9 November 20X3

Subject: Overhead absorption for October 20X3

A significant over absorption arose during the month. The total amount over absorbed was £18,400 compared with total actual expenditure of £15,800.

Could you please check the data for me to ensure that no recording errors have occurred?

The actual production overhead figure may be too low, perhaps because of miscoding of invoices. Alternatively, the activity data for the production departments may have been recorded incorrectly.

Thank you for your help.

TASK 11

Workings for determination of revenue and cost behaviour patterns

Sales revenue

Selling price per case = £28,000/7,000 = £4

Check: 6,200 x £4 = £24,800; 5,900 x £4 = £23,600

Candles cost

Candle cost per case = £9,100/7,000 = £1.30

Check: 6,200 x £1.30 = £8,060; 5,900 x £1.30 = £7,670

Packing materials cost

Packing materials cost per case = £5,250/7,000 = £0.75

Check: 6,200 x £0.75 = £4,650; 5,900 x £0.75 = £4,425

Packing labour cost

Packing labour cost per case = £2,100/7,000 = £0.30

Check: 6,200 x £0.30 = £1,860; 5,900 x £0.30 = £1,770

Packing overhead cost

	Cases	£
High	7,000	5,400
Low	5,900	5,180
Difference	1,100	220

Variable cost per case = £220/1,100 = £0.20. Fixed cost = £5,400 – (7,000 x £0.20) = £4,000

Check: for 6,200 cases cost is £4,000 + (6,200 x £0.20) = £5,240

Other overhead cost

Fixed cost = £2,500 per month

TASK 11, CONTINUED

Quality Candles Limited: mail order division
Planned results for December 20X3

	December
Number of cases to be sold	6,800
	£
Candles cost (@ £1.30)	8,840
Packing materials cost (@ £0.75)	5,100
Packing labour cost (@ £0.30)	2,040
Packing overhead cost	5,360
Other overhead cost	2,500
Total costs	23,840
Sales revenue (@ £4)	27,200
Profit	3,360

Space for workings

Packing overhead cost

	£
Fixed	4,000
Variable (6,800 × £0.20)	1,360
	5,360

TASK 12 (i)

Quality Candles Limited: mail order division

Planned results for December 20X3: increased activity

	December
Number of cases to be sold	7,600
	£
Candles cost (@ £1.30)	9,800
Packing materials cost (@ £0.60)	4,560
Packing labour cost (@ £0.30)	2,280
Packing overhead cost	5,520
Other overhead cost	2,500
Total costs	24,740
Sales revenue (@ £4)	30,400
Profit	5,660

Space for workings

Packing overhead cost

	£
	£
Fixed	4,000
Variable (6,800 × £0.20)	1,520
	5,520

FOULKS LYNCH
PUBLICATIONS

TASK 12 (ii)

Quality Candles Limited: mail order division

Planned results for December 20X3: increased activity

Calculation of breakeven point and margin of safety: working paper

	£	£
Contribution per case:		
Selling price		4.00
Less variable costs:		
Candles	1.30	
Packing materials	0.60	
Packing labour	0.30	
Packing overhead	0.20	
		2.40
Contribution per case		1.60
Fixed overhead:		
Packing overhead		4,000
Other overhead		2,500
		6,500

Breakeven point

Number of cases to break even $= \dfrac{£6,500}{£1.60}$

$= 4,063$ cases

Margin of safety	=	7,600 – 4,063 cases
	=	3,537 cases
	=	**47%** of planned activity

TASK 12 (iii)

INTERNAL MEMO

To: General Manager

From: Bobby Forster, Accounts Assistant

Date: 11 November 20X3

Subject: **Mail order division: bulk discounts for December 20X3**

I have evaluated the proposal to increase sales and take advantage of a bulk discount for packing materials.

The planned profit will increase considerably to £5,660 for the month compared with £3,360 without the increased activity. The breakeven point will be 4,063 cases which results in a margin of safety of 47% of planned activity.

Since the company is looking for opportunities to increase profit, the high profit and the wide margin of safety mean that this represents a very attractive proposal.

However the following assumptions affect the validity of the projections.

•   The increased sales volume can be achieved at the current selling price. It is possible that the selling price would have to be reduced in order to sell the greater output.

•   All other unit variable costs and fixed costs will not be altered by the increase in activity. Since the volume projection is outside the range for which data is available this may not be a valid assumption. For example it may be necessary to pay overtime rates to labour in order to achieve the increased output.

•   The increased volume can be achieved with the existing packing and delivery capacity.

Please let me know if you require any further information.

TASK 13 (i)

Working paper for the financial appraisal of purchase of delivery vehicles

Year	Cashflow	Discount factor	Present value
		£ @ 12%	£
2003	-90,000	1.000	-90,000
2004	34,800	0.893	31,076
2005	34,800	0.797	27,736
2006	34,800	0.712	24,778
2007	39,800	0.636	25,313

Net present value 18,903

Working space for calculation of payback period

	Cumulative cashflow (£)
2003	-90,000
2004	-55,200
2005	-20,400
2006	14,400

Payback period = 2 years + (20,400/34,800 = 2.6 years

TASK 13 (ii)

INTERNAL MEMO

To: General Manager

From: Bobby Forster, Accounts Assistant

Date: 14 November 20X3

Subject: **Purchase of delivery vehicles for mail order division**

The proposal to purchase delivery vehicles is acceptable from a financial viewpoint because it returns a positive net present value of £18,903 at a discount rate of 12%. This calculation assumes that all cashflows occur at the end of each year.

The payback period is between two and three years. If we assume even cashflows during the year the payback period can be calculated as 2.6 years. This is acceptable since it is shorter than the company requirement of three years, although there is not much room for error in the cashflow calculations.

Please let me know if I can help any further with the evaluation.

ANSWERS TO PRACTICE SIMULATION 1

TASK 1

MATERIAL X103 – STORES LEDGER - FIFO								
Date	Materials received			Materials issued			Materials stock		
	Qty	Unit (£)	Value (£)	Qty	Unit (£)	Value (£)	Qty	Unit (£)	Value (£)
1 January							200	4.40	880
5 January				180	4.40	792	20	4.40	88
8 January	400	4.50	1,800				20	4.40	88
							400	4.50	1,800
12 January				120:					
				20	4.40	88			
				100	4.50	450	300	4.50	1,350
20 January	320	4.60	1,472				300	4.50	1,350
							320	4.60	1,472
21 January				220	4.50	990	80	4.50	360
							320	4.60	1,472
25 January				140:					
				80	4.50	360			
				60	4.60	276	260	4.60	1,196
TOTALS	**720**		**3,272**	**660**		**2,956**	**260**		**1,196**

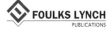

MATERIAL X103 – STORES LEDGER - LIFO								
Date	Materials received			Materials issued			Materials stock		
	Qty	Unit (£)	Value (£)	Qty	Unit (£)	Value (£)	Qty	Unit (£)	Value (£)
1 January							200	4.40	880
5 January				180	4.40	792	20	4.40	88
8 January	400	4.50	1,800				20	4.40	88
							400	4.50	1,800
12 January				120	4.50	540	20	4.40	88
							280	4.50	1,260
20 January	320	4.60	1,472				20	4.40	88
							280	4.50	1,260
							320	4.60	1,472
21 January				220	4.60	1,012	20	4.40	88
							280	4.50	1,260
							100	4.60	460
25 January				140:					
				100	4.60	460	20	4.40	88
				40	4.50	180	240	4.50	1,080
TOTALS	**720**		**3,272**	**660**		**2,984**	**260**		**1,168**

TASK 2

MATERIAL X103 – STORES LEDGER – WEIGHTED AVERAGE								
Date	Materials received			Materials issued			Materials stock		
	Qty	Unit (£)	Value (£)	Qty	Unit (£)	Value (£)	Qty	Unit (£)	Value (£)
1 January							200	4.40	880
5 January				180	4.40	792.00	(180)	4.40	(792.00)
							20	4.40	88.00
8 January	400	4.50	1,800.00				400	4.50	1,800.00
							420	4.495	1,888.00
12 January				120	4.495	539.40	(120)	4.495	(539.40)
							300	4.495	1,348.60
20 January	320	4.60	1,472.00				320	4.60	1,472.00
							620	4.549	2,820.60
21 January				220	4.549	1,000.78	(220)	4.549	(1,000.78)
							400	4.549	1,819.82
25 January				140	4.549	636.86	(140)	4.549	(636.86)
TOTALS	**720**		**3,272.00**	**660**		**2,969.04**	**260**		**1,185.96**

FOULKS LYNCH
PUBLICATIONS

MEMORANDUM

To:	To: Managing Director
From:	From: Cost Accountant
Date:	Date: February
Subject:	**Stock issue pricing**

FIFO, LIFO and weighted average methods of stock pricing all base material issue prices on the actual price paid for the material.

FIFO, or first in first out, uses the material price of the earliest purchases of stock items available. In the stores ledger produced, the issue on the 5th January is priced at £4.40 which is the price of the opening stock. The issue on the 12th January is made up of 20 units at £1.40, the remainder of the opening stock and the other 100 units at £4.50, the price of the first receipt of goods on 8th January. The closing stock of 260 units is valued at the most recent price of goods received, £4.60. LIFO, or last in first out, prices material issues at the most recent price paid for material purchases. Therefore the material issue on the 8th January is priced at £4.50, the price of the most recent receipt of goods. The closing stock of 260 units is valued at the earliest price of unused stock.

In this example this is:

	£
240 at £4.50	1,080
20 at £4.40	88
	1,168

Weighted average price approach calculates an average price of items in stock each time a new receipt is recorded. This price is then used to issue materials to production. Therefore it can be seen that following the receipt on the 8th January a new weighted average price of:

$$\frac{\text{Total Volume in stock}}{\text{Total units in stock}} \quad \frac{£1,888}{420} = £4.495$$

is calculated. This is then used to price the material issue on 12th January. The closing stock of 260 units is valued at the weighted average price of stock remaining.

With reference to your memo the answers to your points are as follows:

1. LIFO follows (typical) physical stock distribution.

    It is in fact a FIFO method that typically follows physical stock distribution. First in, first out is used physically to avoid stock deterioration or obsolescence. Therefore this statement is false.

2. SSAP 9 would tend to support FIFO.

    SSAP 9 supports any issue pricing method felt to give a true and fair view of the underlying business position. As stock issues are often/typically FIFO, physically, FIFO would therefore be a method supported by SSAP 9.

3. Weighted average is capable of providing the most up-to-date and appropriate product costings for determining and setting product selling prices.

    Of the methods cited, in fact LIFO would charge the most up to date costs to production and/or cost of sales and produce the most up to date product prices.

4.   In times of inflation LIFO produces lower balance sheet stock valuations.

LIFO records items coming out of stock at latest prices. Thus items left in stock are recorded at the older, lower, pricings. This statement is therefore true.

5.   In times of inflation FIFO produces lower period profit figures.

FIFO gives lower cost of sales figures than LIFO or the weighted average method and therefore lower prices are charged for issues to production. If cost of sales is lower then in fact profit for the period will be higher than under the other methods.

TASK 3

MEMORANDUM

To:	Jack Small
From:	Cost Accountant
Date:	February
Subject:	**Materials control**

Our recent growth in activity and business size probably warrants a full review of our control of materials purchasing, receipts and issues.

One of our fundamentals, if we are to fully safeguard corporate interests and assets and avoid theft and pilferage, is to implement systems of internal control and check.

In particular, we need to ensure that materials purchasing is properly planned for. Requirements should be closely linked to production and sales needs and alternative choices of suppliers, taking account of quality, supply times and pricing/costs should be considered before decisions are made.

Order quantities and re-order levels (ie, levels to which stocks may decline before new orders are placed) should be set for each material. These in turn will allow us to determine maximum, minimum and average stock levels. Maximum stock levels can be advised to the stores personnel as an audit control. They should never be exceeded. If they are it may mean, for example, that someone in purchasing has ordered too much from a supplier or perhaps that production needs have declined and we need to reduce order quantities in future periods. The minimum stock levels will provide for follow-up with suppliers, if appropriate, following order placement to ensure that deliveries take place in good time to satisfy our production and sales flow. Average stock levels will help us to calculate our costs of carrying or keeping stocks.

Materials control involves using our stock control levels and periodically checking actual material needs, purchasing, and usage with plans.

The main concern of internal check will be division of duties to avoid fraud or theft. Ensuring that different individuals authorise purchases, physically control materials, and record transactions will aid our control and make fraud very difficult without collusion. Purchase orders issued by purchasing should be copied to accounts and stores to record purchases made in the accounts and support subsequent receipts in stores, respectively. If such division is considered carefully it can be seen that no-one in the business will have the opportunity to extract unwarranted cash for purchases without the matter showing up either by store keepers not receiving materials for cash paid as evidenced by purchase orders or materials held in stock not matching up with those evidenced in the records as being purchased.

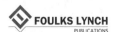

In order to ensure that materials are properly recorded and not misappropriated, documentation should be fully used to support purchasing, receipt and utilisation. As re-order levels are reached, stores should issue a purchase requisition (signed) with copies to purchasing and accounts. When goods are delivered, receipts staff should complete and sign a goods received note (GRN) - taking responsibility for the items they receive and attesting to their quantity and quality. The GRNs should be copied to accounts and purchasing and a copy should be signed by stores and held by the receipts personnel to register stores responsibility for taking the items concerned. As items are issued by stores, persons receiving them should sign materials requisitions to take responsibility for them - stores keeping full copies.

Accounts should only pay for items as invoices arise which are fully supported by purchase requisitions, GRNs and orders.

Finally periodic routine checks should be made to ensure that all personnel are following systems and procedures - internal audit checks should be used for this purpose. The checks could cover physical treatment of items in stores - designed to ensure that deterioration or any other value losses are avoided as far as possible.

TASK 4

Reorder level:

Max usage × Max lead time

= 50 units × 8 days

= 400 units

Maximum stock level:

ROL + ROQ − (Min usage × Min lead time)

= 400 + 1,000 − (30 × 6)

= 1,220 units

Minimum stock level:

ROL − (Average usage × Average lead time)

$$= 400 - (\frac{9,840}{240} \text{ units} \times 7 \text{ days})$$

= 113 units

Average stock level:

1,000/2 + 113 = 613 units

TASK 5

STORES LEDGER/BIN CARD											

| Materials Code | X103 | | | ROL | 400 units | | | Minimum S/L | 113 units | | |
| Item description | S/L Capacitors | | | ROQ | 1,000 units | | | Maximum S/L | 1,220 units | | |

Receipts			Issues			On order					
Date	GRN Ref	Quantity	Date	Req'n Ref	Quantity	Physical balance	Date	Ref	Quantity ($\checkmark$ = rec'd)		
1 Jan						200	31 Dec	I210	400	$\checkmark$	
			5 Jan	22,450	20						
8 Jan	Y504	400				420	8 Jan	I246	320	$\checkmark$	
			12 Jan	22,568	120	300					
20 Jan	Y557	320				620					
			21 Jan	22,691	220	400					
			25 Jan	22,742	140	260					

TASK 6

TIME-BASED PAY	Charles White	Pamela James	Joanne Peters
Normal time working	160 hours	160 hours	160 hours
(4 × 40 hours)			
Overtime hours	12 hours	8 hours	20 hours
Normal time pay	£800	£800	£800
Overtime pay	£90	£60	£150
(£7.50 per hour)			
Totals	**£890**	**£860**	**£950**

FOULKS LYNCH PUBLICATIONS

PIECE-RATE WITH MINIMUM GUARANTEE

	Charles White	Pamela James	Joanne Peters
Piecerate pay			
(60 units £14)	£840		
(50 units × £16)		£800	
(52 units × £12.50)			£650
Minimum guaranteed			
(80% of earlier time - based pay figures)			
(80% × £890)	£712		
(80% × £860)		£688	
(80% × £950)			£760
Payments to be made	£840	£800	£760

TASK 7

Employee:	Charles White	Pamela James	Joanne Peters
Time taken:	172 hours	168 hours	180 hours
Time allowed:			
60 units × 3 hours	180 hours		
50 units × 3.5 hours		175 hours	
52 units × 2.8 hours			145.6 hours
Time saved:	8 hours	7 hours	Nil
Bonus:			
8 hours × £5 × 50%	£20		
7 hours × £5 × 50%		£17.50	
Time-based payments: (from Task 8)	£890	£860	£950
Total wage:	£910	£877.50	£950

TASK 8

MEMORANDUM

To:	Toby Stringer
From:	Cost Accountant
Date:	February 200Y
Subject:	**Payment incentive schemes for labour**

Payment incentive schemes such as a premium bonus and piece rate schemes with a guaranteed minimum are designed to motivate our employees to greater productivity. They generally carry advantages in that:

- higher overall production is achieved - thus providing for greater business profits provided products can be sold.

- labour costs per product unit are generally lower. Bonus schemes ensure payments for production in excess of that expected, so that time is paid for at less per unit than would be expected for production in normal time.

- higher production means better use of the fixed cost investment in production. The same or similar levels of fixed cost payments for resources such as rent, rates, and plant and machinery (via depreciation) allied to higher production means a lower fixed cost per unit of product.

- labour morale is higher and employees are highly motivated.

Drawbacks may exist however in that:

- quality may suffer (safeguards on quality must be built into any incentive scheme);

- higher productivity may result in higher material waste.

Incentive labour schemes may not be appropriate or workable where:

- quality is important or imperative;

- employees have no definable or consistent units of output or have no control over the efficiency of output (e.g. where machines produce units at a regular rate outside employee control);

- markets for output are limited and there are no real benefits to excessively high production levels.

The potential for payment incentive schemes should be considered in the light of these points.

TASK 9

Overhead recovery rates

Costs Centre	Assembly 1		Assembly 2		Packing	
Total overhead	£65,500		£50,500		£47,500	
Direct labour hours	8,500		8,000		7,500	
Overhead recovery rate	£7.71	Per direct labour hr	£6.31	Per direct labour hr	£6.33	Per direct labour hr

TASK 10

Production cost schedule '57' mini radio-CD player

	£
Direct labour:	
4.5 hours × £5/hr	22.50
Direct materials:	
3 units × £4.50	13.50
2 units × £2.50	5.00
Production overhead:	
Assembly 1 2hrs × £7.71	15.42
Assembly 2 2.25hrs × £6.31	14.20
Packing 0.25hrs × £6.33	1.58
	£72.20

TASK 11

Cash flow		Year 1	Year 2	Year 3	Year 4	Year 5
		£	£	£	£	£
	£(25,000)	7,000	8,000	9,000	7,500	7,500
NPV factor	1.0	0.870	0.757	0.658	0.573	0.498
NPV	£(25,000)	6,090	6,056	5,922	4,298	3,735

Net present value   £1,101

ANSWERS TO PRACTICE SIMULATION 2

TASK 1

MEMORANDUM	
To:	Managing Director
From:	Cost Accountant
Date:	31 January 200X
Subject:	**Cost accounting terminology**

Below is a brief summary of the terms and concepts that have caused some concern.

Direct and indirect costs

Direct costs are the costs that can be specifically identified as the direct input costs of a product.

For example the materials used in a product are direct materials. The cost of the labour working on the product is a direct labour cost. Any expenses such as royalties or copyrights that can be directly identified with each product are direct expenses.

Indirect costs are other expenses of the business that although necessary in order to make the products cannot be directly identified with an individual product.

For example the oil used to lubricate machinery is a cost of making the products but as its cost cannot easily be assigned to each individual product, it is described as an indirect material cost. The salary of the production supervisor cannot be assigned to each product as he does not actually make any products but supervises those that do work on the products. Therefore his salary is an indirect labour cost. Most expenses such as factory rent, rates, heat and light are also indirect costs as they will rarely be able to be identified with a particular product.

Variable and fixed costs

Variable costs are those that vary in amount directly with the quantity of production.

Fixed costs are those that are stable and do not vary with the amount of production.

For example the cost of materials used in a product will increase or decrease as the amount of that product produced increases or decreases. This is a variable cost. However the rent of the factory building will remain the same for the period whatever the level of production. This is a fixed cost.

Are all variable costs direct and all fixed costs indirect?

Variable costs such as materials and labour usually tend to be direct costs. However there might be some exceptions such as the oil used in the machinery as this will vary with the level of production but is usually classified as an indirect cost.

Fixed costs by definition do not vary with the amount of output therefore fixed costs are usually indirect costs.

Overheads

Overheads is simply another term for indirect costs. Therefore indirect materials, indirect labour and indirect expenses are all overheads.

Allocation, apportionment and absorption

These terms all relate to overheads. Any overheads that can be specifically assigned to a department or area of the business (known as a cost centre) are said to be allocated to that cost centre. For example the salary of the production manager for production department A will be an overhead that is allocated to production department A.

Any costs that are shared by a number of cost centres must be apportioned in some fair manner between each of the relevant cost centres. For example the rent of the building that houses the production department and stores must be apportioned between these two departments.

Finally when all overheads have either been allocated or apportioned to the relevant departments or cost centres they must then be split amongst the products that the production departments make. This is known as absorption of overheads into product costs. For example if the total overhead for production department A is £10,000 then this must somehow be absorbed into the cost of the units produced by production department A in the period. The method of absorption will depend upon the organisation's policies.

Semi fixed and semi variable costs

Semi fixed costs and semi variable costs are two alternative names for a specific type of cost. This is a cost that is partly fixed and partly variable. For example a telephone bill includes a fixed element that is the rental charge and a variable element that is the charges for the calls actually made.

TASK 2

	Machine hours of activity in production	Power costs £
High activity:	410	29,200
Low activity:	280	21,400
Difference:	130	7,800

Variable cost per machine hour: £7,800 ÷ 130 = **£60**

Estimate of fixed costs: £29,200 – (£60 × 410) = **£4,600**

Projections for 200X: Fixed costs (total): £4,876
(£4,600 × 1.06)

Variable cost per machine hour: £63.60
(£60 × 1.06)

TASK 3

Overhead allocation and apportionment schedule

Overhead	Basis	Assembly £	Finishing & packaging £	Canteen £	Repairs £	Total £
Rent	Floor area	18,667	3,733	800	800	24,000
Rates	Floor area	3,733	747	160	160	4,800
Insurances	55:35:5:5	1,925	1,225	175	175	3,500
Power costs	Machine hours	27,419	2,133			29,552
Heating and lighting	Floor area	2,956	590	127	127	3,800
Canteen supplies	Allocated			1,250		1,250
Depreciation	Allocated	3,400	1,050			4,450
Production supervisor	Employees	10,667	1,333			12,000
Repairs	Allocated				5,600	5,600
Other allocated costs	Allocated	8,600	2,100			10,700
Budgeted overhead		77,367	12,911	2,512	6,862	99,652
Reapportionment of service costs:						
Canteen	Employees	2,116	264	(2,512)	132	
Repairs	Machine hours	6,489	505		(6,994)	
Budgeted production overhead		85,972	13,680			99,652

All figures rounded to nearest full £.

OARs are then computed as:

Assembly   £23.88 per machine hour (£85,972 ÷ 3,600)

Finishing & packaging   £3.72 per labour hour (£13,680 ÷ 3,680)

Note: that due to rounding you may have small differences in your own computations.

TASK 4

PRODUCTION COST SCHEDULE 200X

			£
Costs:	Labour		8.00
	Materials		6.50
	Overhead:	Assembly (0.25 hrs × £23.88)	5.97
		Finishing & packaging (0.75 hrs × £3.72)	2.79
			23.26

Machine hrs: 0.5 (0.25 in Assembly)

Labour hours in Finishing & packaging 0.75

TASK 5

Over/under absorption of overheads

Assembly

	£
Actual overhead	82,600
Absorbed overhead	
3,350 hours × £23.88	79,998
Under absorption	2,602

Finishing & packaging

	£
Actual overhead	15,540
Absorbed overhead	
3,700 hours × £3.72	13,764
Under absorption	1,776

Production overhead control account - assembly

	£		£
Bank/creditors	82,600	WIP (Absorbed) (3,350 × £23.88)	79,998
		P/L (under absorbed)	2,602
	82,600		82,600

Production overhead control account - finishing and packaging

	£		£
Bank/creditors	15,540	WIP (Absorbed) (3,700 × £3.72)	13,764
		P/L (under absorbed)	1,776
	15,540		15,540

MEMORANDUM

To:	Managing Director
From:	Cost accountant
Date:	31 January 200X
Subject:	**Overhead absorption**

When a unit of a product is being produced it is reasonably easy to determine at the time of its production the amount of materials included in the product and the amount of labour hours spent working on the product. However the situation is different with overheads. It would, for example, be difficult to determine how much actual electricity went into each unit or how much of the canteen costs.

However it is important that the total cost of a unit of product is known for pricing and planning purposes. Therefore, as well as planning the precise amount of materials and labour to be included in a unit, the amount of variable and fixed overheads to be included in the cost must also be planned in advance. This is then the total standard cost of the unit.

In order to produce this standard cost before the variable and fixed overheads have actually been incurred it is necessary to calculate the anticipated amount of each overhead, allocate and apportion these to the relevant production and service departments and then reapportion any service department costs to the production departments. At this point the expected amount of production overhead for each production department is then known and this will be apportioned to the anticipated number of units to be produced in that production department in some manner.

This is what is known as a pre-determined overhead absorption rate and it is necessary if the total cost of a unit of a product is to be estimated in advance of its actual production.

The actual amount of variable and fixed overheads will only be known at the end of the period under review. The actual number of units produced will also only be known at the end of the period.

If either of these figures, actual overhead or actual units produced, is different from the figures used to calculate the overhead absorption rate at the beginning of the period then there will be an under or over absorption.

If the actual amount of overhead is higher than anticipated but production is as expected then there will be an under absorption of overhead. This will be because the amount absorbed will be based upon the smaller budgeted overhead rather than the larger actual amount.

If the overhead for the period is as expected but production levels are higher than budgeted then there will be an over absorption of overhead. This will be because the pre-set overhead absorption rate will be applied to a higher amount of production.

There are of course other combinations of overhead differences and production differences that can lead to under or over absorption but I hope that these examples have explained where such an over or under absorption comes from.

Any amount of overhead that is under absorbed has by definition not been included in the cost of work in progress. However it is an actual cost that has been incurred by the organisation and therefore its accounting treatment is to write it off as an expense in the profit and loss account.

Any amount of overhead that has been over absorbed is an amount that has been included in work in progress but has not in fact actually been incurred. As such it must be added back to profit and this is done by the over absorption being credited to the profit and loss account as a reduction of expenses.

I hope that you will now be able to see how the overhead budgeted for and actually incurred affects product costs and the overall profit and loss. The product costs to be included in work in progress, finished goods and cost of sales will be based upon the amount of overheads absorbed into the products on the basis of the pre-set overhead absorption rate. Therefore whatever happens to the actual variable and fixed overheads throughout the period the product cost remains the same.

Any overhead that is either understated (under absorption) or overstated (over absorption) is corrected in the profit and loss account as a separate debit or credit entry.

TASK 6

Labour turnover

		Production workers	Non-production workers
200V		$\dfrac{0}{8}$	$\dfrac{2}{5}$
	=	0%	40%
200W		$\dfrac{5}{15}$	$\dfrac{4}{8}$
	=	33%	50%

Comment:

- The numbers of employees are so small that it will be difficult to draw too many meaningful conclusions.

- Were there any major differences in production technology, working conditions or management between 200V and 200W in order to cause such differences in labour turnover?

- Was 200W just a particularly unusual year in that the high number of production leavers was due to unavoidable causes such as illness, injury or leaving the area?

- Why were the turnover levels amongst non-production workers so high each year? Again was this due to unavoidable reasons such as illness, moving area, pregnancy etc?

- Were working conditions or management particularly poor during 200V and 200W in order to cause such high levels of labour turnover amongst non-production workers?

- What reasons were given by the employees who left for leaving?

TASK 7

MEMORANDUM

To:	Production manager
From:	Cost accountant
Date:	31 January 200X
Subject:	**Depreciation**

The objective of depreciation is to charge a part of the cost of each fixed asset to the products that the asset makes, and therefore to the profit and loss account, each period. The reason for this is that the fixed assets, largely machinery in the production departments, are used in order to make the products in just the same way as the materials, labour and other overheads are used to make the products.

If the machinery is being used to make the products then it is only right that some amount should be charged to the products to reflect this use. This amount is known as depreciation.

There are a variety of methods by which an asset can be depreciated. None are more correct than others although some may be more suitable in different situations.

The main aim of depreciation is to charge a certain amount of the initial cost of a machine to the products each period. The most straightforward way of doing this is to charge the same proportion or percentage of the initial cost of the machine to the products in each period. This is known as the straight line method of depreciation.

An alternative is to use the reducing balance method of depreciation. This method charges a higher amount of depreciation in the early years of an asset's life than in the later years. This reflects the fact that many assets lose much of their value in early years of their life and less in later years, such as cars. The way in which reducing balance depreciation is calculated is to apply a constant percentage each year to the net book value (or cost less depreciation to date) of the asset.

Finally a method of depreciation that may be of use in machine based departments is the machine hour rate. Under this method the total number of hours of a machine's life is initially estimated. The depreciation charge for the period is based upon the proportion of those total hours that the machine has been used in that period, applied to the initial cost of the machine.

TASK 8

New Product 'X7' CD Player

	£ (per unit)
Selling price	70
Variable cost	30
Contribution	40

Break-even point in units

$$= \frac{\text{Fixed costs}}{\text{Contrlbution per unit}}$$

$$= \frac{£65,000}{£40}$$

$$= \quad 1,625 \text{ units}$$

Margin of safety

$$= \quad 5,000 - 1,625$$

$$= \quad \underline{3,375} \text{ units}$$

FOULKS LYNCH
PUBLICATIONS

ANSWERS TO PRACTICE SIMULATION 3

TASK 1

STORES LEDGER ACCOUNT

Material description: Timber (10 metre lengths)

Code No: T10

Date	Receipts			Issues			Stock balance		
	Quan-tity	Price £ per lengt	Total £	Quan-tity	Price £ per length	Total £	Quan-tity	Price £ per length	Total £
1 March							50	17.50	875.00
4 March	200	18.00	3,600.00.00				50	17.50	875.00
							200	18.00	3,600.00
							250		4,475.00
8 March				150	18.00	2,700.00			
							50	17.50	875.00
							50	18.00	900.00
11 March	500	15.75	7,875.00				100		1,775.00
							500	15.75	7,875.00
							600		9,650.00
13 March				350	15.75	5512.50	50	17.50	875.00
							50	18.00	900.00
							150	15.75	2362.50
						437.50	250		4137.50
15 March				25			25	17.50	437.50
				50	17.50	900.00			
				150	15.75	2,362.50			
				225		3,700.00	25		437.50

18 March	100	20.25	2025.00				25 100	17.50 20.25	437.50 2025.50
							125		2,462.50
22 March				80	20.25	1620.00	25 20	17.50 20.25	437.50 405.00
							45		842.50

TASK 2

MEMO

To: Stuart York

From: Tracy Green

Date: 3 April 2002

Subject: **Economic Order Quantity**

The economic order quantity for timber depends on three main factors

- ordering costs

- storage costs

- trade discount.

Referring to my calculations on the attached appendix you will see that total ordering costs fall as order size increases whilst storage costs increase. Purchase costs fall in a series of stages which reflect the different levels of trade discounts.

Based on the assumptions given, the economic order quantity is that which minimises the total of the costs incurred. This is at an order size of 400.

I recommend, therefore, that orders are placed for a quantity of 400 each time if we are to change from the current weekly review system to a fixed order level system. This will require a re-order level to be set such that stock-outs are minimised.

If you require any further information please do not hesitate to contact me.

TASK 2

Appendix to Memorandum

Order size	Number of orders placed during year	Ordering cost £	Storage cost £ (W1)	Purchase cost £ (W2)	Total cost £
100	100	2,000	525	202,500	205,025
200	50	1,000	1050	180,000	182,050
300	33.3	600	1575	180,000	182,175
400	25	500	2100	157,500	160,100
500	20	400	2625	157,500	160,525
600	16.7	334	3150	157,500	160,984
700	14.3	286	3675	157,500	161,461
800	12.5	250	4200	157,500	161,950

Note: You will get slightly different figures if you have chosen to round the number of orders placed during a year to a whole number.

(W1)   For an order size of 100 storage cost is $\dfrac{100}{2} \times 10.50 = £525$ etc.

(W2)   For an order size of 100 a 10% trade discount applies thus purchase cost is

$100 \times £22.50 \times 90\% = £2,025$ per order
$\times 100$ orders placed in a year
_____
£202,500

TASK 3

Timesheet	Week ending		6 March 2002
Employee name	Ron O'Sullivan	Employee number	23
Department	Machining	Employee grade	1

Activity	Monday Hours	Tuesday Hours	Wednesday Hours	Thursday Hours	Friday Hours	Total Hours
Machining	10	6	6		8	30
Waiting for work		2	2			5
Sick				8		8
Training					2	2
Discrepancy						
Total hours payable for	10	8	8	8	10	44
Number of covers produced	70	51	62	0	62	
Standard time for units produced	700	510	620	0	620	
Time taken	600	360	360	0	480	
Time saved	100	150	260	0	140	
Bonus payable	6.67	10.00	17.33	0	9.33	4.33

Signed	Ron O'Sullivan		Manager	Amy Rowel

Analysis for week	Rate per hour £	Hours	Wages cost £
Direct wages	30	8.00	240.00
Indirect wages			
Basic hours	15	8.00	120.00
Overtime premium	2	8.00	16.00
Bonus	–		43.33
	47		419.33

Timesheet   Week ending   6 March 2002

Employee name   Jim Davis   Employee number   56

Department   Assembly   Employee grade   2

Activity	Monday Hours	Tuesday Hours	Wednesday Hours	Thursday Hours	Friday Hours	Total Hours
Assembly	7	10	4		4	25
Holiday			4	8		12
Waiting for work	1					1
Training					4	4
Total hours payable for	8	10	8	8	8	42
Number of covers produced	65	72	30	0	32	
Standard time for units produced	585	648	270	0	288	
Time taken	420	600	240	0	240	
Time saved	165	48	30		48	
Bonus payable	8.94	2.60	1.63	0	2.60	15.77

Signed   Jim Davis   Manager   Amy Rowel

Analysis for week	Rate per hour £	Hours	Wages cost £
Direct wages	25	6.50	162.50
Indirect wages			
Basic hours	17	6.50	110.50
Overtime premium	1	6.50	6.50
Bonus	–		15.77
	43		295.27

COST LEDGER DATA ENTRY SHEET

Week ending   6 March 2002

     Debit accounts

	Cost centre Code	Expenditure code	Amount to be debited £
	10	07	240.00
	20	07	162.50
	30	07	
	40	07	
	50	07	
	10	08	179.33
	20	08	132.77
	30	08	
	40	08	
Check total: total wages for the two employees	50	08	
			714.60

TASK 4

MEMO	
To:	Stuart York
From:	Tracy Green
Date:	10 March 2002
Subject:	**Group bonus schemes**

A group bonus scheme is where the bonus is based upon the output of the workforce as a whole or particular groups of the workforce. So in our company appropriate groups may be the different production cost centres. The bonus is then shared between the individual members of the group on some pre-agreed basis, for example shared equally or pro-rata to basic wages.

A group scheme is considered to have the following advantage over individual schemes:

- group loyalty may result in less absenteeism and lateness

- it is an easier system to administer as only total output for the department need be recorded

- it may be appropriate where the work is carried out by teams.

However all members of the team are rewarded regardless of the effort they make. This may be demotivating to efficient, hard working employees if less efficient workers are rewarded equally. It may also limit the level of bonus that the more efficient workers can achieve.

TASK 5

MEMO

To:	Stuart York
From:	Tracy Green
Date:	2 April 2002
Subject:	**Basics for Overhead Absorption**

The purpose of overhead absorptions is to allocate overhead to cost units on a basis which fairly reflects the amount of overhead incurred by each cost unit

In labour intensive departments, such as the assembly department, as many of the overheads are associated with the number of direct labour hours, for example holiday pay, sick pay and idle time, it is considered most accurate to absorb overhead on the basis of direct labour hours.

In machine intensive departments, such as the machining department, overheads are mainly machine related, for example maintenance and repair costs. Therefore machine hours are considered to be the fairest method to absorb overhead.

There are numerous other methods, which can be used. In the packing department we use a unit basis. This is most appropriate when each unit uses the same amount of overhead.

Using different bases may appear complicated but results in much more accurate product costs when products pass through different departments incurring different types of overhead. If, however, products are similar it may be possible to simplify the process and use a common overhead rate for all three departments without significantly affecting the accuracy of costs. Perhaps we could test the impact of such a change on a number of sample products and determine to what extent change would impact on the accuracy of the final product cost, before we reach a final decision for the system to be used for next years budget.

TASK 6

OVERHEAD ANALYSIS SHEET: 2002/03

Overhead expense: Primary apportionments and allocations	Basis of allocation/ apportionment	Total £	Assembly Dept £	Machining Dept £	Packing Dept £	Stores £	Canteen £
Rent and rates	Floor area	125,000	48,077	33,654	24,038	11,058	8,173
Canteen	Number of	32,000	17,390	4,870	8,580	696	464
Machine maintenance	Quotation	6,000		60,000			
Depreciation on machines	Cost of machines	166,930	2,300	157,000	5,080	1,700	850

Production manager's salary	Time spent	30,000	10,000	10,000	10,000		
Storekeeper's salary	Allocation	20,000				20,000	
Canteen staff	Allocation	18,000				18,000	
Other overheads	Even	60,000	20,000	20,000	20,000		
Total		511,930	97,767	285,524	67,698	33,454	27,487
Re-apportion canteen	Number of employees		15,159	4,244	7,478	606	(27,487)
Total		511,930	112,926	289,768	75,176	34,060	–
Re-apportion stores	Material requisitions		12,800	11,364	9,896	(34,060)	–
Total		511,930	125,726	301,132	85,072	–	–
Direct labour hours			120,000				
Machine hours				80,000			
Production units					450,000		
Overhead absorption rate for 2002/03			£1.05 per direct labour hour	£3.76 per machine hour	£0.19 per unit		

TASK 7

Working sheet for calculation of overhead under/over absorbed

Assembly department, quarter ending 30 June 2002

Production overhead absorbed   32,500 × £1.05   £134,125

Actual production overhead incurred

£133,250

Production overhead under or over absorbed,   £875 over absorbed
to be transferred to profit and loss account

TASK 8

Investment appraisal

New cutting machine

Payback period

		Cash flow	Cumulative
		£	
YR	1	30,000	30,000
	2	40,000	70,000
	3	25,000	95,000
	4	20,000	115,000
	5	20,000	135,000

Payback period

$$= \quad 2 \text{ years} + \left(\frac{5,000}{2,500} \times 12 \right)$$

$$= \quad \underline{2 \text{ years 3 months}}$$

NPV Schedule

		(Outflow)	Inflow	NPV factor	NPV
YR	0	(75,000)		1.0	(75,000)
	1		30,000	0.870	26,100
	2		40,000	0.757	30,280
	3		25,000	0.658	16,450
	4		20,000	0.573	11,460
	5		20,000	0.498	9,960
				NPV	£19,250

TASK 9

Marginal cost analysis

New production line code 'XX125'

	£
Selling price per unit	90
Variable cost per unit	50
Contribution per unit	40

Break-even point in units

$$= \frac{\text{Fixed costs}}{\text{Contribution per unit}}$$

$$= \frac{£75,000}{£40}$$

= 1,750 units

Margin of safety in units

= 6,000 – 1,750 = 4,250

% of planned output

ANSWERS TO SPECIMEN EXAMINATION

TASK 1.1

STOCK CARD								
Product: Pink plastic								
	Receipts			**Issues**			**Balance**	
Date	Quantity kgs	Cost per kg £	Total cost £	Quantity kgs	Cost per kg £	Total cost £	Quantity kgs	Total cost £
							10,000	10,000
b/f 1.11.03								
6.11.03	20,000	1.10	22,000				30,000	32,000
11.11.03				16,000	10,000 × 1.00 6,000 × 1.10	10,000 6,600 16,600	**14,000**	**15,400**
17.11.03	10,000	1.20	12,000				**24,000**	**27,400**
19.11.03				20,000	14,000 × 1.10 6,000 × 1.20	15,400 7,200 22,600	**4,000**	**4,800**

TASK 1.2

Date	Code	Dr	Cr
6 Nov	1000	**22,000**	
6 Nov	3000		**22,000**
11 Nov	1000		**16,600**
11 Nov	1100	**16,600**	
17 Nov	1000	**12,000**	
17 Nov	3000		**12,000**
19 Nov	1000		**22,600**
19 Nov	1100	**22,600**	

TASK 1.3

Normal rate	12,000 hours x £6	=	£72,000
Overtime premium	1,400 hours x £3	=	£4,200
Total direct labour cost		=	**£76,200**

TASK 1.4

Fixed overheads for November	Basis	Total £	Warehouse £	Manufacturing £	Sales £	Accounting £
Depreciation	Net book value	7,400	1,665	4,995		740
Rent	Floor space	2,500	375	1,750	250	125
Other property overheads	Floor space	3,200	480	2,240	320	160
Accounting overheads	Allocated	6,250				6,250
Staff costs	Allocated	18,925	4,230	3,015	6,520	5,160
		38,275	6,750	12,000	7,090	12,435

TASK 1.5

Budgeted fixed overhead absorption rate = £12,000/20,000 = £0.60

TASK 1.6

Product: Meg doll	£
Direct costs	
Pink plastic	39,200
Direct labour	76,200
Indirect costs	
Manufacturing department overheads	7,200
Total cost of production	122,600
Number of Meg dolls produced	36,000
Unit cost of production (to the nearest penny)	3.41

SECTION 2

TASK 2.1

Product	E	C	R
	£	£	£
Selling price per unit	30.00	40.00	60.00
Less: Unit variable costs			
Direct materials	10.00	11.00	12.00
Direct labour	16.00	16.00	20.00
Variable overheads	2.00	1.75	7.00
Contribution per unit	2.00	11.25	21.00

TASK 2.2

Number of units = £4,800/£2 = **2,400 units**

TASK 2.3

Use the data from Task 2.1 to complete the table below.

Product	E	C	R
Contribution per unit	£2.00	£11.25	£21.00
Machine hours per unit	0.1	0.15	0.35
Contribution per machine hour	£20.00	£75.00	£60.00

TASK 2.4

The products should be ranked by contribution per limiting factor, in this case machine hours. The ranking is as follows:

1   Product C

2   Product R

3   Product E

Total available machine hours = 365 hours. Based on the ranking above:

Use **225 hours** to manufacture **1,500 units of C**

Use **140 hours** to manufacture **400 units of R**

No units of E should be manufactured.

TASK 2.5

(a)

The payback period required to recoup an investment of £80,000 from one year is as follows:

From year two	£15,000	Outstanding investment	£65,000
From year three	£25,000	Outstanding investment	£40,000

In year four, the product generates £80,000, so the extra time needed to pay back the investment is six months.

Total payback period is **two years and six months**.

(b)

	Year 1	Year 2	Year 3	Year 4	Year 5
	£000	**£000**	**£000**	**£000**	**£000**
Design costs	(80)				
Sales revenues		30	50	160	50
Variable costs		15	25	80	25
Net cash flows	(80)	15	25	80	25
Present value factor	0.909	0.826	0.751	0.683	0.621
Present value	(72.7)	12.4	18.8	54.6	15.5

Net present value = £28,600

TASK 2.6

REPORT		
To: Managing Director	From: Candidate	Date: Dec 03

The net present value technique relies on discounting relevant cashflows at an appropriate rate of return. It would be helpful to know:

1   Whether there are any additional cashflows beyond year five.

2   Whether the introduction of a new product will affect sales of the existing products E, C and R.

On the basis of the information provided, the project has a positive net present value of £28,600 and should be carried out.

AAT Order Form

4 The Griffin Centre, Staines Road, Feltham, Middlesex, TW14 0HS, UK.
Tel: +44 (0) 20 8831 9990 Fax: + 44 (0) 20 8831 9991
Order online: www.foulkslynch.com Email: sales@ewfl-global.com

For assessments in 2003/2004		Textbooks		Workbooks		Combined Textbooks/ Workbooks	
Foundation stage – NVQ/SVQ 2							
1 & 2	Receipts and Payments	£10.95	☐	£10.95	☐		
3	Preparing Ledger Balances and an Initial Trial Balance	£10.95	☐	£10.95	☐		
4	Supplying Information for Management Control					£10.95	☐
21*	Working with Computers					£10.95	☐
22 & 23#	Achieving Personal Effectiveness and Health & Safety					£10.95	☐
Intermediate stage – NVQ/SVQ 3							
5	Maintaining Financial Records and Preparing Accounts	£10.95	☐	£10.95	☐		
6	Recording and Evaluating Cost and Revenue	£10.95	☐	£10.95	☐		
7	Preparing Reports and Returns	£10.95	☐	£10.95	☐		
8 & 9	Performance Management, Value Enhancement and Resource Planning and Control	£10.95	☐	£10.95	☐		
Technician stage – NVQ/SVQ 4							
10	Managing Systems and People in the Accounting Environment	£10.95	☐	£10.95	☐		
11	Preparing Financial Statements	£10.95	☐	£10.95	☐		
15	Cash Management and Credit Control	£10.95	☐	£10.95	☐		
17	Implementing Auditing Procedures	£10.95	☐	£10.95	☐		
18	Business Taxation FA 2003	£10.95	☐	£10.95	☐		
19	Personal Taxation FA 2003	£10.95	☐	£10.95	☐		

* Unit 21 can be taken at Foundation Level or Intermediate Level

\# Unit 23 can be taken at any level

Postage, Packaging and Delivery (Per Item):

	First	Each Extra
UK	£5.00	£2.00
Europe (incl ROI and CI)	£7.00	£4.00
Rest of World	£22.00	£8.00

Product Sub Total £..................	Post & Packaging £.................	Order Total £....................	(Payments in UK £ Sterling)

Customer Details

☐ Mr ☐ Mrs ☐ Ms ☐ Miss Other ....

Initials:.................................. Surname: ....

Address: ....

....

....

Postcode: ....

Telephone: ....

Email: ....

Fax: ....

Delivery Address – if different from above

Address: ....

....

Postcode: ....

Telephone: ....

Payment

1   I enclose Cheque/PO/Bankers Draft for £......................................
     Please make cheques payable to '**Foulks Lynch**'.

2   Charge MasterCard/Visa/Switch a/c no:

Valid from: ☐☐☐   Expiry date: ☐☐☐

Issue No: (Switch only)

Signature: .... Date: ....

Declaration

I agree to pay as indicated on this form and understand that
Foulks Lynch Terms and Conditions apply (available on request).

Signature: .... Date: ....

Notes: Prices are correct at time of going to print but are subject to change

Delivery please allow:
United Kingdom	– 5 working days	
Eire & EU Countries	– 10 working days	
Rest of World	– 10 working days	

Notes: All orders over 1kg will be fully tracked & insured.
Signature required on receipt of order. Delivery times
subject to stock availability.

FOULKS LYNCH PUBLICATIONS